# *The*
# Compound
# Code

Scott G. Kyle & Patrick B. Fischer

# *The* Compound Code

## An Expert Guide to Trading Stocks & Options

Liv Mas Press

Published by LIV MAS Press

Scott Kyle (CEO) & Patrick Fischer are financial advisors at Coastwise Capital Group, LLC, an SEC registered investment advisor. The authors do not intend to provide personalized investment advice through this publication and do not represent that the securities or services discussed are suitable for any investor. Investors are advised not to rely on any information contained in the publication in the process of making a fully informed investment decision.

This publication is designed to provide accurate and authoritative information regarding the subject matter covered. It is sold with the understanding that neither the authors nor the publisher is engaged in rendering legal or accounting service. If legal advice or other expert assistance is required, the services of a competent professional person should be sought.

Many of the contents of this book are based on *The Power Curve – Smart Investing Using Dividends, Options, & The Magic of Compounding*. The contents of this book have been updated to reflect the most current information available at the time of publication.

Library of Congress Cataloging-in-Publication Data available on request. ISBN 978-0-9778018-2-4

A C E G I K J H F D B

Library of Congress Control Number:

Hardcover: 978-1-64184-897-8
Paperback: 978-1-64184-898-5
Ebook: 978-1-64184-899-2

First edition

Printed in the United States of America

# DEDICATIONS

*To my amazing kids, Jet and Liv, the best return on investment I ever made. And to my gorgeous and brilliant wife Victoria who always challenges and inspires me to be the best version of myself.*

*—Scott*

*To my wonderful children, Reese and Pierce, fondly known as Crazypants and Wildman, respectively. And to my wife Lillian Cheng, the deepest thanks for supporting me in pursuing my creative passions.*

*—Patrick*

# CONTENTS

# PREFACE

In the last two decades, much in the world of markets and finance has changed while other aspects of investing remain constant. Interest rates as measured by the 10 Year Treasury dropped to an all-time low of 0.318% in 2020, and trillions of dollars of negative interest rate bonds were purchased around the world. While yields rallied somewhat in the following years, the historic decline in rates put savers in a tough spot and placed a premium on finding real, reliable, sustainable sources of income.

On the options front, the number of contracts traded exploded to over 10 billion for the first time ever in 2022 from just over 1 billion 10 years earlier according to CBOE/FIA. In early February 2023, a single day record of over 68 million options contracts changing hands was reached. Clearly professional and amateur investors alike had become aware of the potential power of using options to speculate, protect, and perform other useful functions in their portfolios.

At the same time, many investing themes that existed ten or twenty years ago ring ever true today. Just as newbie investors with little experience rushed into the market to speculate on things with which they had little experience or expertise, so to have we seen newfangled options products lure novices with dreams of getting rich quick, only to lose much of their capital in the blink of an eye. One such well known turbo charged options related product lost 95% of its value in one day and shut down entirely shortly thereafter, leaving its holders scratching their heads and opening empty wallets.

An eerie resemblance to the 2007-2009 era took hold in the early 2020s when companies with weak balance sheets were forced to cut or eliminate their dividends, leaving those relying on this income in dire financial straits. Not to mention shells of companies in the form of SPACs being promoted by celebrities cashing out early while retail investors ultimately held an essentially worthless bag. These developments – or more aptly echoes of history – put a premium on the greatest risk to every investor: **_knowing what you are doing_**.

More than ever before, the themes detailed in _The Compound Code: An Expert Guide to Trading Stocks & Options_ are essential for every investor to successfully navigate inevitable stormy market waters.

In straightforward and accessible language, _The Compound Code: An Expert Guide to Trading Stocks & Options_ reveals the power behind dividend-paying companies and sophisticated options trading techniques in a way that can lead to superior income and long-term profits. While most investment books are either largely academic or entertainment oriented—technical analyses or biographies of the world's great investors—_The Compound Code_ offers a practical, easy-to-understand, and immediately applicable guide to investing that was previously the purview of Wall Street hedge-fund hotshots. As with most things in life, success is driven by both science (technical proficiency) as well as art (the learned ability to do things well). The goal of this book is to provide you with both the art and the science necessary for you to achieve superior stock returns over time and to benefit directly from the power of compounding.

# CHAPTER 1

## THE IMPORTANCE AND POWER OF COMPOUNDING

Historically speaking, equities are one of the best asset classes when it comes to providing returns in excess of inflation over time. For those with a very long time horizon and no inclination to be involved in portfolio management, a passive index fund approach is perfectly suitable for obtaining market like returns. However, investors who have pools of money with a less than a 'buy and hold forever' time horizon, the time, desire, as well as the ability (which we seek to teach you in this book), can tap into the benefits an active trading program may provide. These include enhancing income beyond yields like those offered by the S&P 500, reducing volatility, and potentially outperforming the market. Regarding the latter, let's look at the difference in seemingly small return variations over time shown by Figure 1.1.

Two accounts each starting with $100,000 will have dramatically different balances twenty or even ten years later with one account earning a seemingly small two or three additional percentage points per year on average. This is the power of compounding at work. Incremental differences that would not get your attention in the near term can mean the difference between having to extend your working years and retiring early with security, or the difference between taking a cruise and owning a yacht. Investor holding periods are often a lot longer than realized. Even if you are investing for retirement five, 10 or 15 years away, the money must still last another 10 – 30 years or more beyond that. So returns matter over time, especially long investment periods. With that in mind, there are often several year intervals when individual stocks, or the market as a whole, go approximately nowhere. There can be many ups and downs along the way (volatility that you can take advantage of in a profitable way), but a buy-and-hold strategy during these periods would have left your brokerage account essentially flat, especially when you factor in inflation. Adding even a small level of intelligent trading can help get you up the return curve, which, over the years, can make a material impact on the size of your account.

Among the four major sources of stock-related gains - long-term capital appreciation, dividends, short-term trading, and income from the sale of options—the latter three sources can add reliable incremental gains. The goal is to show you how to make the most of the market's natural fluctuations and to profit from the magic of compounding.

*Figure* **1.1 Return Variations over Time**

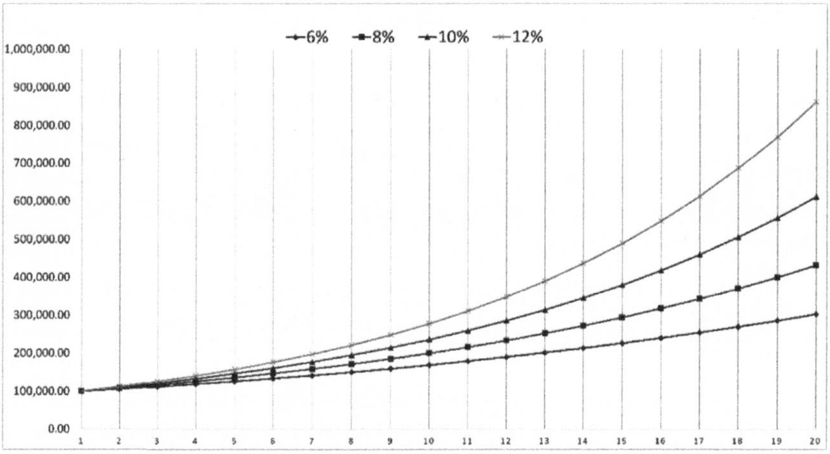

*"Compound Interest is the Most Powerful Force in the Universe."*

Certainly, one of the world's great investors must have uttered this weighty and telling quote. Was it the wise and venerable Warren Buffett? Perhaps the irascible but entertaining Jim Cramer? The legendary and honored Ben Graham? Actually, it was not an investor at all, but a scientist, a particularly famous and important one at that. The man who proclaimed that compounding was more powerful than gravity, electromagnetism, or even atomic friction was none other than Albert Einstein.

Let's look at this force in action.

**_Figure_ 1.2 Logarithmic Representation of Compounding**

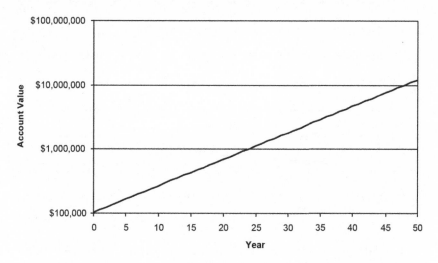

In this representation on Figure 1.2 the vertical axis is skewed so that a given distance always represents the same percentage change. (This means that the distance between 10 and 100 is the same as between 100 and 1,000 since each represents a tenfold growth, although the absolute gains of going from 100 to 1,000 are clearly greater). You will occasionally see stock-gain charts that use this methodology. Do not be fooled by this mathematically correct optical illusion! The more representative gains are shown by Figure 1.3.

As you can see from the figure, the power of compounding kicks in as time goes on. Investment gains (annual percentage returns) may appear at first glance to improve over time since the chart seems to be flat in the early years and to go higher in later years. In reality, it is the power of compounding 'doing its thing' in subsequent years that makes these gains so large on an absolute basis.

*Figure* **1.3 Linear Representation of Compounding**

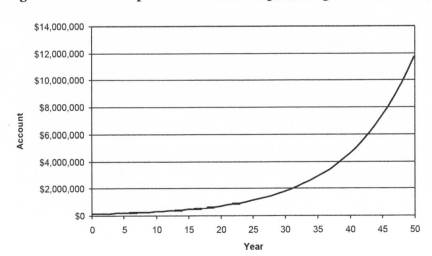

Let's do some basic math. Your account starts out at $100,000. In the first year you make 10%, or $10,000. Now your account is worth $110,000. In year two you make another 10%, bringing your total account value up to $121,000. (You made 10% not only on the original $100,000 but also on the $10,000 from year one, yielding total year two profits of $11,000). In year three you make another 10%, in this case $12,100, and so on. By the end of year ten your account is up to $259,374; by the end of year twenty your account is worth $672,750. By Year twenty-six, the amount of gains *per year* exceeds the original investment amount. The power of compounding has taken hold.

Few people appreciate – or have the patience to benefit from the fact that - even small differences in returns can have a dramatic impact on account balances over time as compounding works its mathematical magic.

Now that we know how the power of compounding aids in wealth creation, let's see how we can best tap into this force in the equities and **options** markets.

# CHAPTER 2

## THE ROLE OF DIVIDENDS IN EQUITY RETURNS

Throughout various times in history, dividend-paying stocks have gone out of vogue while capital gains (stock appreciation) ruled. Multi-year periods of underperformance by quality, dividend-paying companies are generally exceptions in the history of the U.S. stock market. Studies show dividends have been responsible for between 40% and 50% of total returns that stocks have provided over the last 100-plus years. Read that again: *Around half of the returns that stocks have yielded over the decades have come from dividends.*

After stock bubbles, dividend-paying stocks generally come back into style with a vengeance. Investors who were seeing strong capital gains suddenly disappear become interested in the reliable income and greater stability generally associated with dividend-paying stocks. Investors were attracted by more than regular checks in the mail and capital gains potential. While there have certainly been periods in recent history when non dividend paying growth stocks have outperformed, multiple studies indicate that over long periods, dividend-paying stocks have provided superior *total* returns over their non-dividend–paying brethren.

To be sure, not all dividend-paying companies are the same. Given the importance of dividend-paying stocks in one's portfolio construction, and with so many income-oriented vehicles to choose from, what should investors look for when considering which companies to purchase?

First some basics. A company's **dividend yield** (aka **yield**) is the amount of dividends paid on a per share basis divided by the company's stock price. For example, if a stock is trading at $40 per share and the company pays an annual dividend (most pay dividends quarterly, so multiply the quarterly dividend by four) of $2 per share, the stock has a dividend yield of 5%. The yield changes, by mathematical definition, with movement in the stock price as well as an increase or decrease in the dividend paid. An increase in stock price absent a commensurate increase in dividend will lower the yield. An increase in the dividend combined with a flat stock price will raise the yield. As we will discuss in more detail below, a company's stock price decreasing, thus causing its dividend yield to increase dramatically, can be a sign of problems and the stock should be watched with a critical eye.

The next thing to know is the company's **payout ratio**. This is simply the dividend on a per share basis divided by **earnings per share (EPS)**. If a company pays out $2 per share annually and has earnings of $4.50 per share, the company's payout ratio is approximately 44%. This is a very important statistic as it indicates how likely the company is to continue to pay, or to increase, its dividend over time. A payout ratio of less than 50% is preferable. If a company's payout ratio starts getting north of 70% due to a decline in earnings, this is a sign that the dividend may ultimately be cut.

*Figure* **2.1 History of Payout Ratios**

| | Year | | | | | | | | |
| | 2015 | 2016 | 2017 | 2018 | 2019 | 2020 | 2021 | 2022 | 2023 |
|---|---|---|---|---|---|---|---|---|---|
| **Dividends** (per share) | $0.49 | $0.58 | $0.68 | $0.80 | $0.84 | $0.89 | $0.94 | $0.99 | $1.05 |
| **Earnings** (per share) | $1.51 | $1.76 | $2.06 | $2.41 | $2.10 | $1.83 | $1.59 | $1.38 | $1.20 |
| | | | | | | | | **DANGER ZONE** | |
| **Payout Ratio** | 32.36% | 32.64% | 32.92% | 33.20% | 40.26% | 48.82% | 59.20% | **71.79%** | **87.06%** |

As noted in Figure 2.1, Company X continued to raise its dividends even as earnings started to decline in 2019. The result is an increase in the payout ratio. As the payout ratio climbed above 70% in 2022, it served as a warning sign that Company X might cut its dividend because the company is not well positioned to pay out that kind of cash to shareholders.

Companies *hate* cutting their dividend and Wall Street investors despise seeing companies cut their dividends even more than companies hate reducing them. If a company declares a cut in its dividend, you can be confident that the stock price will fall as a result. Don't think for a minute, however, that a struggling company won't cut its dividend. While reluctant to do so, companies take this kind of negative financial action all the time.

There are four important events around the dividend payment: the **dividend declaration date**, **the dividend record date**, the **dividend ex-date**, and the **dividend payment date**. The declaration date, or announcement date, is the day on which the next dividend payment is declared by the board of directors of the company. Typically, companies follow regular schedules when announcing each quarterly dividend. The record date is the date used to determine which shareholders are entitled to the dividend or distribution. The ex-date is the first date on which the stock trades without its dividend payment. In order to receive a stock dividend, you must buy a stock prior to the ex-date. This will ensure that you are a shareholder of record for receipt of the dividend. If you buy the stock on the ex-date or after, you will not be entitled to the announced dividend. Alternatively, if you own the stock and want to sell your shares but still receive the dividend, you must sell on or after the ex-date. Stock prices tend to drop on the ex-date by the amount of the dividend to be paid. For instance, if a company is paying a dividend of $0.50 per share, on the ex-date its stock price will drop by $0.50 in addition to any normal market movement that day. This is simply because the company has taken a piece of itself, namely $0.50 per share of cash on its **balance sheet** and set it aside to send to investors as a dividend payment. Thus, all things being equal, the company is worth $0.50 per share less on the ex-date than it was on the day before the ex-date, and it trades accordingly. Sophisticated quote systems will even indicate that a stock is up on its ex-date if it falls by less than its dividend payment amount. For example, a stock that drops from $40 to $39.80 on the day it goes ex with an anticipated $0.50 per share dividend payment might be indicated to have gone up 0.75% ($0.30 divided by $40) that day. This makes sense as the investor has not lost money; instead, his holdings have merely been rearranged. Finally, the payment date is the date when accounts are actually credited with the dividend, or the checks are mailed to those who receive dividends directly rather than having them applied to brokerage accounts.

**Figure 2.2 Dividend Payment Schedule**

| Automatic Data Processing, Inc. (ADP) | | | |
|---|---|---|---|
| **Jan. 11, 2023**<br>Dividend Declaration<br>of $1.04 | **March. 9, 2023**<br>Dividend Ex -Date | **March. 10, 2023**<br>Record Date | **March. 31, 2023**<br>Pay Date |

SOURCE: NASDAQ.COM

## WHY DIVIDENDS MATTER AND WHY INCREASING DIVIDENDS COUNT EVEN MORE

It is important to remember that the payment of a dividend is not necessarily a good thing in and of itself. It is a taxable event for non-qualified accounts in which the company gives a piece of itself back to the investor to spend, invest elsewhere, or put back into the company paying the dividend, typically via a dividend reinvestment plan. If, for example, a company is paying a $1 dividend and is trading at $50 per share, the stock will drop by $1 per share to $49 per share on the ex-date, barring additional market movement. The investor's account now contains $49 worth of stock and $1 worth of cash, the $1 distribution being taxable. Your $50 of stock before the dividend payment is now $49 of stock, $0.85 of cash and $0.15 in the pockets of the IRS for those in the 15% dividend tax bracket. Doesn't sound like such a great deal now, does it? So why do you hear commentators praising dividends? Clearly it is the company's ability to keep paying dividends that matters, since ultimately there is a direct correlation between ever-increasing dividends and ever-increasing earnings, the latter of which tends to lead to ever-increasing stock prices over time. Management that knows it has to cut a big check to shareholders every ninety days—and a bigger check every 365 days for those companies that consistently increase their annual dividend payments—will create a culture in which increasing earnings are a priority. In order to fulfill this mission dividend-paying companies tend to outperform the market over time because management has this extra incentive to exercise financial discipline that favors stockholders. Cutting a dividend is tantamount to admitting failure, and these companies have set their bars high.

Let's look at the example of AbbVie Inc. (ABBV) as evidence of the long-term correlation between dividends, earnings, and stock price. As of 2022, ABBV paid an annual dividend of around $5.71 per share and had earnings of approximately $13.84 per share. The company had a 10-year run from 2013 to 2022 with cumulative dividend growth of 256% and earnings up 340%. Though the payout ratio fluctuated over the years, it largely ranged between 40%-60%. These figures show the strong long-term correlation of earnings and dividend growth for companies which increase their dividends consistently over time.

## VERIFYING THE SOURCE OF YIELD

There is good yield and there is bad yield. It is vitally important to always know the difference, but especially in market environments where product marketers are pushing and investors are reaching for yield, often stretching so far that they fall off the proverbial tree branch. If you hear from analysts or Wall Street pundits something along the lines of, "I don't think the company is going anywhere any time soon, but it has a 5% dividend, so I get paid for waiting," then you are being misled. Some additional background is in order.

Many investors believe dividends are paid out of earnings. They are not; dividends are paid out of cash. A company can have no earnings or earnings that are less than a given dividend payment, and the company can still make its declared payout as long as it has the cash to do so—either cash on its books or access to cash via credit facilities (read: debt). It is a consistent increase in earnings that allows a company to increase its dividend over time. (Note that to minimize the amount of arcane accounting under consideration we can simply interchange **cash flow** and earnings that, for companies in most industries, approximate each other over time). Often periodicals such as the *Wall Street Journal* (WSJ) will print a table of high-yielding securities—stocks, closed-end funds, and the like—ranked by highest yield.

You will occasionally find listed companies and funds yielding 10% or more. It is very important to dig deeper to determine the source of this yield. There are two major red flags that you should look for. The first, as noted above, is when a company is paying out more than it is earning. If its payout ratio is over 100% for several quarters running, then that is exactly what you should be doing, too. To state the obvious, this scenario is not sustainable. A company cannot finance forever a dividend payment through borrowing. If you find a company yielding north of 6%, look carefully at its payout ratio. In most cases it will be at 70% or more, the dividend subject to reduction in the near term. Stay away from these companies as the last thing you want to do is buy into a company just before it slashes its dividend.

Another scenario for a high-yielding security is a fund, usually closed end, that makes a so-called 'controlled payout.' An example would be a fund trading at $10 per share fixing its dividend payout at $1.30 per share so that the fund yields 13%. Sounds like a great deal, right? Headlines blare: HOW WOULD YOU LIKE TO MAKE 13% INCOME? In most cases, however, the fund or the underlying securities it holds are not earning enough to cover the dividend (which is often referred to as a 'distribution' since it may not technically be a dividend at all), thus the fund is simply returning principal to shareholders. In other words, the fund is taking money you gave to them and returning it slowly to you over time and charging you a fee for the pleasure. In doing so, the fund is returning to shareholders the very thing the shareholders are counting on to create an income stream. *This is the bad kind of yield.* Buying $10 worth of a security only to have 13% - or some large portion - of it given back to you annually in a taxable event is not an optimal investment approach.

Think of what this means in the long term. Let's say someone advertised an investment that guaranteed a 20% annual dividend stream. You give them $100 and for five consecutive years they hand you back $20. If they are not earning more on the original money than they are returning to you in the form of a 'dividend' then eventually the money runs out and the game is over. The 20% yield provided a total return **on investment (ROI)** of precisely 0% and a negative ROI after taxes. When a company is paying back more than it is earning, the dividend yield will rarely make up for the capital loss, and your total position return may be negative.

Do not confuse a strong dividend with superior returns *per se*. They usually do correlate over time, but a strong balance sheet can mask operational weakness in the midterm. The investor must look at what is behind the yield. Is the company or fund earning more than it is paying back in the form of distributions? Is its payout ratio comfortably south of 60% and holding steady or better yet declining? If yes, all is fine. If not, then the yield is artificially high, and the payout will likely be trimmed down, or principal is being paid out, or both, leaving the investor with inferior returns.

*It is not the fact that a company does pay a dividend that is meaningful, but the fact that it can.* Read that sentence again because it contains one of the most important concepts in dividend-stock investing.

## Compelling Dividend Ranges

If having too much yield is potentially a bad thing, where are the sweet spots for dividend stocks? The optimal yields fall into two areas depending on investor objectives: (1) growth dividend companies that typically have yields ranging from 1% to 3%, and (2) income dividend companies with yields often in the 3% to 6% range. We will also discuss emerging dividend companies that recently started paying a dividend and/or have a yield of under 2% but are poised to increase their dividend substantially over time.

There are many growth dividend companies that have paid and increased their dividends for decades. The Dividend Aristocrat list is a good starting point for companies such as these. At the same time, they are typically companies with good underlying growth rates while investing in their organic expansion with the cash not paid out to investors. These growth dividend companies have characteristics that include: (1) a low payout ratio, typically under 30%-40%, because they tend to be investing a lot in their future growth and thus choose to hold on to much of their excess cash for internal growth purposes; (2) high-dividend-growth rates, often in excess of 8% - 12%; and (3) strong financials including high profitability and a solid balance sheet.

These are the companies that can give you both capital appreciation and income gains over time.

Growth dividend companies are the kinds of stocks you buy for your young kids' college education—and the income generated by the reinvested dividend payments fifteen years hence could potentially pay for a good chunk of the tuition, with the stock likely providing capital gains to boot.

Compare growth dividend companies with classic income dividend companies paying out 3% to 6% yields. The latter would generally include the usual suspects like financials, telecoms, and pharmaceuticals. These companies are characterized by higher yields (often in excess of the yield on the ten-year Treasury), higher payout ratios (usually over 40% but still ideally under 80%), annual dividend growth in the 2% to 6% range, and strong financials. These are the kinds of companies that will be slow but steady growers, with less capital gains potential than their growth dividend company peers but with a very strong income potential. You can build a high-quality portfolio of companies from a wide variety of industries with yields in the 2% to 6% range that will satisfy both your current and future income needs and provide good capital gains potential as well. The key is to be patient and let the power of compounding take hold over time.

## EVER-INCREASING DIVIDENDS AND COMPOUNDING

As will be discussed further in chapter 3, a company's ultimate worth is a function of the discounted cash flows it generates and either pays out in the form of dividends or reinvests in operations for future earnings growth. While your yield at purchase may seem paltry, by taking advantage of ever-increasing dividends—not to mention reinvesting them—you can have a meaningful **effective yield**, which is defined as the current dividend divided by the original stock purchase price.

Even if dividends are not reinvested, an investor's effective yield on a security that is increasing its dividend regularly does increase over time. As noted in Figure 2.3, effective yield increases to nearly 8% in ten years for a stock that has a 3% yield at time of purchase and increases its dividend at a rate of 10% per year on average.

*Figure* 2.3 Numerical Calculations of Effective Yield Without Dividend Reinvestment

| Year | Share Price | Number of Shares No Reinvesting | Annual Div/Share | Effective Yield |
|------|-------------|--------------------------------|------------------|-----------------|
| 0 | $100.00 | 2000 | $3.00 | 3.00% |
| 1 | $105.00 | 2000 | $3.30 | 3.30% |
| 2 | $110.25 | 2000 | $3.63 | 3.63% |
| 3 | $115.76 | 2000 | $3.99 | 3.99% |
| 4 | $121.55 | 2000 | $4.39 | 4.39% |
| 5 | $127.63 | 2000 | $4.83 | 4.83% |
| 6 | $134.01 | 2000 | $5.31 | 5.31% |
| 7 | $140.71 | 2000 | $5.85 | 5.85% |
| 8 | $147.75 | 2000 | $6.43 | 6.43% |
| 9 | $155.13 | 2000 | $7.07 | 7.07% |
| 10 | $162.89 | 2000 | $7.78 | 7.78% |

Let's review how effective yield grows when dividends are reinvested. In this case, the investor reinvests dividend payments every quarter, and the shares purchased with last quarter's dividends produce even more yield in the future.

In Figure 2.4, assuming the stock price increases at a rate of 5% per year, effective yield has increased to over 11% after ten short years. Of course, what your effective yield will turn out to be is dependent on both the annualized rate of increase of the dividend payment and the price at which additional shares have been purchased. As counterintuitive as it may seem, the stock price going down in the early years increases effective yield in future years as more shares are purchased on which future dividends will be paid—a natural form of dollar cost averaging.

*Figure* 2.4 Numerical Calculations of Effective Yield with Dividend Reinvestment

| Year | Share Price | Number of Shares With Reinvesting | Annual Div/Share | Effective Yield |
|------|-------------|-----------------------------------|------------------|-----------------|
| 0 | $100.00 | 2000.00 | $3.00 | 3.00% |
| 1 | $105.00 | 2057.14 | $3.30 | 3.39% |
| 2 | $110.25 | 2118.72 | $3.63 | 3.85% |
| 3 | $115.76 | 2185.15 | $3.99 | 4.36% |
| 4 | $121.55 | 2256.94 | $4.39 | 4.96% |
| 5 | $127.63 | 2334.61 | $4.83 | 5.64% |
| 6 | $134.01 | 2418.78 | $5.31 | 6.43% |
| 7 | $140.71 | 2510.14 | $5.85 | 7.34% |
| 8 | $147.75 | 2609.46 | $6.43 | 8.39% |
| 9 | $155.13 | 2717.63 | $7.07 | 9.61% |
| 10 | $162.89 | 2835.65 | $7.78 | 11.03% |

You can clearly see the power of compounding when it is applied to the reinvestment of dividends over time. When you start, the movement is not so dramatic. But as the yield begins to increase and gains momentum, it really starts taking off...to the point where its own momentum keeps it going over time. The last part of that sentence, "over time," is the key. You have to stay in the game to get the benefit of compounding. This is the most difficult part; not putting the brakes on before dividends have had the chance to really accelerate.

## FOCUSING ON THE HIGHEST QUALITY SECURITIES

The importance of having quality dividend-paying companies as a core part of your portfolio is a lesson easily forgotten when times are good, but economies and financial markets inevitably hit tough spots. Cash is king. Cash is real. Dividends are real. High quality dividend paying companies may not double in price overnight, but build a portfolio of companies like these, buy them when valuations are reasonable (see Chapter 3 on stock valuation), focus your energy elsewhere, and the excitement and potential wealth building associated with quality dividend-paying stocks will emerge over time. You can take that to the bank.

The key to being a great investor is to always remember that a storm is just around the corner—you just don't know when it will hit or how severe it will be—and to prepare accordingly. Owning quality dividend-paying stocks as a core part of your portfolio is a great way to have an umbrella at your side, especially during the 100-year storms that inevitably hit every three to five years.

Simply put, if you find a company that has consistently raised its dividend 10%+ year after year, then you have very likely found a company that has also consistently increased its earnings 10%+ year after year. Earnings growth does not have to precisely match dividend growth, but over the years, the two statistics of earnings and dividend growth will generally mirror each other. Most companies that have paid dividends consistently for years have their financial houses in order. So, when the *merde* hits the fan and equities are getting pummeled, high-quality dividend stocks will generally outperform. Why? Because when the market waters are rough, investors seek companies that have strong earnings, strong balance sheets, and a dividend yield that creates a floor in the stock price—companies that are mature, have a dominant position in their industry, and that can weather the storm.

Key Takeaways:

- Dividends in and of themselves are not necessarily a good thing, but they can be a leading indicator of a strong company.
- Look for companies that pay increasing dividends at a relatively consistent payout ratio.
- Growth dividend companies usually pay out 1%-3% whereas income dividend companies typically pay out 3%-6%+.
- Be patient and let the power of compounding work its magic over time.

# CHAPTER 3

## FUNDAMENTAL ANALYSIS, EQUITY VALUATION, AND OTHER STOCK SELECTION CRITERIA

Just as you must analyze the superficial appeal of high dividend yields, you also must do your basic equity research. Options are simply derivates, their value being a function of the underlying security. Before we look at options, let's take a moment to understand fundamental equity analysis and stock valuation as this is the basis for all superior investing.

When it comes to equity analysis and stock selection, you should take the following into consideration: (1) fundamental company analysis, (2) macroeconomic analysis, (3) technical analysis, (4) demographic analysis, and (5) industry analysis. Given the importance of fundamental analysis, we will address this first and then consider the other four main variables in superior stock selection.

### GRABBING TIGER BY THE TAIL: THE VALUE OF FUTURE EARNINGS

How much would you pay for the future earnings of Tiger Woods, Serena Williams, Patrick Mahomes, Mikaela Shiffrin, or another top performer during his or her prime? This may sound like an unusual question, but it gets to the heart of investing. Say a top athlete decided to put his future career earnings up for sale (not unlike how certain musical artists have sold their future royalties using what are commonly known as 'Bowie Bonds' named after the Thin White Duke who helped to pioneer this security). How would you value that? How much would you pay? As a start, you would assess how much that person has made in the past—from endorsements, competition winnings, and so on. You would then project how much he is likely to make in the future. Will he continue his winning ways? Will the competition catch up to him and his earnings decrease? Will the sport become more or less popular, and will that have an impact on salaries, prize money, sponsorship deals, and the like?

After this kind of analysis, you would come up with estimates of likely earnings over the expected remaining years of a given career. Suppose this range is $120,000,000 to $175,000,000. After factoring in and making assumptions (interest or cap rate, and the number of years) about the time value of money (the fact that a dollar today is worth more than a dollar will be in five years), you might value that career in today's dollars between $55,000,000 and $70,000,000 depending on your interest rate/return assumptions. If you were offered those future earnings for $20,000,000, you would get out your checkbook faster than you can say "hole in one" or "game, set, match." If the ask was $200,000,000 for future winnings, you would probably pass in favor of a more attractive investment.

This is, in essence, the process of stock evaluation, except that in terms of companies we usually think of earning on a per share basis. Often new investors confuse price and value. How so? An investor sees a stock price of $5.70, down from $8.20, and concludes that the stock is cheap. But if the same investor were told that the total **market capitalization** of the company is $300,000,000, and that the company earns only $2,000,000 from barely growing revenues of $50,000,000, he would gain a much clearer sense of how truly expensive the company is. You will, at times, hear commentators say, "Oh, I can buy that stock for about the same price as a cup of coffee, therefore it is cheap." That is missing the point. A $400 stock might be cheap and a $4 stock expensive; what matters is the total company valuation relative to its earnings, sales, margins, earnings growth rate, and other important financial metrics. Whether on a total or a per share basis, whether for a top athlete's career earnings or for a company you are considering putting in your portfolio, the valuation process is the same: analyze historical earnings, project future cash flows, and assess competitive threats and industry trends.

*The real question is: When is the best time to make an offer for future earnings? When is the time to grab the tiger by the proverbial tail?*

The financial analysis behind good stock picking is the easy part. There are plenty of people with sufficient IQs who can do the math. Most investors trip up, however, when they let the right sides of their brains dominate their left sides. Once you have a handle on valuing future earnings, when are you most likely to be offered the greatest return on investment opportunity? After an athlete has just won her seventh tournament in a row and everyone thinks she is unstoppable? Plenty of people would now be willing to pay a big premium for her future career earnings as they extrapolate recent history far into the future. Or do you make an offer after a performance set back? Assuming you do not see any fundamental flaws with the athlete, you would wait for that unusual opportunity when people were questioning the athlete's skills. Because you have followed her career closely and know the recent poor performance is an aberration, you have a high level of comfort taking advantage of this transitory situation to buy future earnings at a discount rather than when she is coming off a winning streak and the price associated with future earnings is high.

The discipline necessary to wait for a temporary moment of weakness and then to attack *sans* emotions (but with the confidence that you know the investment well and that the current dip is aberrational in nature) is at the heart of superior investing. Those who behave in the opposite way—becoming interested in a given opportunity only after it has made headlines as an investment that can do no wrong, invariably do most of their buying high and their selling low - and underperform the market commensurately. The winner in investing is the one who pays the lowest price for the highest-quality company. These opportunities can come with broad market declines or news specific to the company. If the latter, the price drop is usually accompanied by Wall Street analyst downgrades (after the stock has already dropped). In any case, make sure to follow the 'three-day rule' which suggests waiting at least three days before making any stock purchases. Your intention is (or should be) to own the company for years, so a few days of analysis before you pull the trigger is wise. Most declines last for a period of time before the stock bottoms out, so be patient to find your entry point.

Because a company has an ongoing value—an indefinite life—investors are willing to pay a **multiple** of projected earnings rather than merely paying for expected earnings over a given period of time, as would be the case if we bought an athlete's future winnings. How much of a multiple are investors inclined to pay and why? This depends largely on growth rates (top and bottom lines) and profit margins. If a company is increasing its top and bottom lines at 30% per year, an investor might be willing to pay 35 times earnings, whereas the same investor might be willing to pay only 15 times earnings for a company growing at 10% per year. Similarly, investors will tend to pay a higher multiple for a company with large operating margins than for a company with low profit margins. Market valuations also affect individual stock multiples. If the overall market is frothy and/or interest rates very low, investors are typically willing to pay higher multiples of earnings to own a given company's future cash streams.

*Figure* 3.1 **Impact of Variables on P/E Ratios**

|  | Low Growth | High Growth |
|---|---|---|
| **High Margin** | Intermediate P/E Ratio | High P/E Ratio |
| **Low Margin** | Low P/E Ratio | Intermediate P/E Ratio |

Superior returns are achieved when you can find high-margin, high-growth businesses trading at relatively low P/E ratios.

Opportunities to find such a combination do not come around often, but they do periodically.

## PEG RATIOS

By comparing **price/earnings ratios (P/E)** with earnings growth ratios, we can get apples-to-apples comparisons as to how expensive a given company is on an absolute and relative basis. This concept is known as the **price/earnings growth ratio**, or **PEG ratio**. The PEG ratio simply compares a stock's price earnings ratio to its expected earnings per share growth rate. If a company's stock has a P/E ratio of 30× but is growing EPS at 35% per year, its PEG is 0.86 (30/35). Another company might have a lower P/E of 25× but an earnings growth rate of only 10% per year, giving it a PEG of 2.5. Generally speaking, a lower PEG is better as it means you are paying less for earnings growth. PEG is especially valuable for high-growth companies that might appear to be very expensive on a purely P/E basis but that might be more reasonably priced when earnings growth rates are factored in. Of course, those growth rates must be sustained; a company can see its PEG skyrocket with a decrease in its earnings growth rate. PEG is just one of many valuation tools used to determine whether a company is both a great company and a great stock.

## FACTORING IN BROAD MARKET P/E RATIOS

Several excellent books such as *Bringing Down the House* and *Fortune's Formula* have told the stories of people who developed card-counting systems in blackjack that allowed them to beat the house. The simple version of this concept is that the player counts the number of face cards that have been dealt. The fewer the number, the more likely that a face card will be dealt on the next hand and therefore the higher the 'count' is. The higher the count, the more the player should bet on the next hand. The lower the count, the less he should bet. By placing large bets when the count is favorable and smaller bets when the count is unfavorable, the player can maximize his returns. This is pure statistics, plain and simple.

Approaching the stock market as though it were a casino is a misleading way to look at investing. The market's primary purpose is to facilitate financing for corporations and to give investors in turn the opportunity to own pieces of publicly traded companies and receive sufficient returns on their investments over time. But few people know there is an automatic 'count' when it comes to making so-called bets in the stock market. What is this count? It is called the price earnings multiple of the market. Here's how it works. The lower the count, the more likely an investor is to have a winning hand over time (i.e., to make money); the higher the count (the P/E ratio) of the market when an investor puts money into an S&P 500 fund for example, the more likely the investor is to receive inferior returns over time. The same applies to the individual stocks that make up the market as a whole.

A well-known example is from early 2000, when the count or P/E ratio for the S&P 500 was over 40×, making it one of the absolute worst times to make an investment. Virtually every face card had already been shown, and the probability of a winning hand any time soon was very low. After a long and bumpy ten years, an investor in the S&P 500 would still not have made money on his initial investment between 2000 and 2009. Compare this with time periods when the count for the S&P 500 was in the single digits. Returns provided by the market over the subsequent years were far more favorable. In 1982 the broad market P/E ratio was well under 10× and the following decade and a half was one of the best performing periods for equities in history.

The reason the average investor vastly underperforms the market—study after study shows that the typical mutual fund investor made less than half the broad market gains over long periods—is that he invests more money on average when the count (i.e., the P/E ratio) is high and less money when the count is low—either for the market at large, for a given region/sector, or for an individual security. Investors do the exact opposite of what they should do to optimize their returns. Why? Because that is how most people are mentally wired. Many investors start paying attention to stocks only after the positive news has made headlines and is already reflected in prices. When the market drops, this investor decides to sell. Then, after the market has rallied and he starts feeling comfortable with equities again he puts money back into the market. It does not help that the major brokerage firms that advise millions of clients have consistently recommended the sale of stocks after they have gone down and advocated buying stocks after they have already had a great run. Similarly, general market commentators advise that investors should "wait for more clarity"—and a rise in the market—before putting money to work after the market has managed to shoot a bogey. Emotionally this might be the comfortable thing to do, but financially it is investing suicide.

The time to buy future career earnings is after the athlete has experienced a temporary bad spell and everyone has written him off as having his best days behind him. Great companies will actually invest in themselves via stock buybacks when they are experiencing temporary hard times. When you own a quality company at a historically low P/E ratio, the increased **operating earnings** of the underlying business, combined with an expanding P/E multiple in general, can lead to superior gains over time. For that reason, pay close attention to the count. When the market is dealing you a great hand—even though it might look like the casino is on fire—that is when you press your bets. When the count is high, when the market is frothy, that is the time to take some winnings off the table by using some of the trading techniques described in this book. You will eventually be dealt a better investing hand; just be patient. Those face cards still exist in the deck, and you will be amazed that they eventually reappear with regularity. This type of behavior on the margin is what leads to better-than-market returns with lower risk applied.

It takes mental discipline and strength to place your investment 'bets' when the market is going down, bleeding red for seemingly endless periods, while headlines and financial pundits proclaim the end of equities. To be sure, you are likely to be 'wrong' in the near term as it is impossible to call an exact bottom, and trends tend to last longer than your gut tells you they should. But it is when the market is down, when the P/E count is low, that you are most likely to make money in the following three, five, or ten years.

## THE SINGLE HABIT OF HIGHLY EFFECTIVE INVESTORS—ANOTHER LOOK AT THE COUNT

In *The 7 Habits of Highly Effective People,* Stephen R. Covey discusses the idea of creating a matrix with 'to do's' that fall into one of four quadrants: not important and not urgent, not important and urgent, important and not urgent, and important and urgent. Most people, he suggests, focus on things that are not important but rather happen to be in the person's face—e-mails that pop up and so on.

Similarly, highly effective investors have habits that separate them from less successful investors. Very few investors are born with these behavioral traits—the appropriate mindset, discipline, long-term thinking, and the like—and most need to learn them, or to 'un-learn' bad investing habits. Here is a simple construct that will help get you 90% of the way to making good investment decisions and, more important, to avoiding bad ones.

Draw a square and divide it into four quadrants. Label the top row of the large square 'good stock,' the bottom row 'bad stock,' the top left half-hand column of the square 'good company,' and the right-hand column of the square 'bad company.' Now we have a matrix with the upper left quadrant being 'good company/good stock,' the upper right-hand quadrant being 'good stock/bad company,' the lower right-hand quadrant being 'bad stock/bad company,' and the lower left-hand quadrant being 'good company/bad stock.'

*Figure* **3.2 Framework for Investment Quality**

|  | **Good Company** | **Bad Company** |
|---|---|---|
| **Good Stock** | Best<br><br>1 | Second Worst<br><br>3 |
| **Bad Stock** | Second Best<br><br>2 | Worst<br><br>4 |

A company that has consistently made profits, that has a strong balance sheet, and that is a leader in its industry has the characteristics of a 'good company.' A 'good stock' is one whose price of the stock relative to the value of the company is favorable using, for example, the P/E ratio.

The goal of a highly effective investor is to reside in the 'good company/good stock' quadrant. The next best quadrant is 'good company/bad stock.' 'Bad company/good stock' is a little worse, and the place where you do not want to be is the 'bad company/bad stock' quadrant.

Coca-Cola (KO) is a prime example of a good company/bad stock in the late 1990s. It consistently increased its profits from 2000 to 2008; yet in 2008 its stock was down approximately 50% from its high in the late 1990s. Why? Simply put, while KO was still a great company, it was a bad stock when it was selling more than 70X earnings (compared to approximately 15X in 2008 when it was both a great company and a great stock). The stock was too expensive to provide adequate returns in the short or medium term; its count was unfavorable. As a great company, KO was eventually able to reclaim its previous highs around 15 years later, sooner when factoring in reinvested dividends which continued unabated during this period. KO has a strong franchise, it is in a good industry, and the company has a rock-solid balance sheet. None of these factors has changed or will likely change for years. The price you have to pay for this greatness, however, changes from time to time. Catch Coca-Cola or other strong companies when they are both good companies *and* good stocks, and you will increase your chance for good investment returns over reasonable time periods.

## POWER TIP
### Being There

The market at large, not to mention individual securities, can produce well over a typical year's worth of gains in a very short period. Witness Starbucks (SBUX) sporting a chart flatter than hour old latte foam from 2015 to 2018, the stock floating around $60 during this prolonged period. Then, faster than a barista can misspell your name, the stock exploded higher, nearly doubling shortly thereafter. This large well-established company saw its stock price increase by several years' worth of gains in a few months' time. The key is you have to be there for the gains. Spikes in stock prices invariably come when you least expect them, when things look the bleakest, *when emotionally it is the toughest time to own stocks.* But that is when the real dollars are made.

Do not forget that the fundamentals of a business do not change day-to-day with swings in the market price. When you are feeling apprehensive about your holdings, adopt the perspective of the company as opposed to the stock. Ultimately, you own a piece of the business. It is the performance of the company that matters over time, and the stock price will eventually reflect the company's financial fundamentals.

## ADDITIONAL CRITERIA FOR STOCK SELECTION

Now that we have reviewed the components of stock valuation and key fundamental indicators, let's examine the more refined criteria an investor should consider when selecting stocks for a portfolio. While every investor needs to develop his own set of variables to fit his investment knowledge and style, some important metrics to consider are dividend-payment measurements including duration, number of years payment has increased, and payout ratio. Let's also look at profitability metrics including ROI, ROE, return on assets (ROA), return on sales (ROS), and other industry-relevant measures as well as capital structure soundness including balance-sheet strength and debt ratios.

When it comes to dividends, a history of five years or more of heightened dividends is a good place to begin your research. For income dividend companies, 2%-5% annual increases should be the minimum. For growth dividend companies, dividend growth rates closer to 10% or more should be viewed favorably. In terms of the payout ratio, a company that has consistently paid out less than 70% of its earnings in the case of high-yielding stocks and less than 40% in terms of lower-yielding **growth stocks** is a good starting point. If you see the payout ratio jump and stay high, this is a warning sign of earnings challenges at the company and further investigation is warranted.

An investor must also consider several important valuation metrics, depending on the type of industry that the investment target is in. The most widely examined valuation metric, and certainly a good place to begin our discussion, is that of the price/earnings ratio, or P/E. P/E ratios should be compared to the company's historical P/E range, to those of the company's peers, to the market as a whole, and to the company's growth (PEG ratio). A lower P/E ratio, combined with a favorable (as in low) PEG ratio, makes for a good investment candidate. For example, if Company X is trading at 13× earnings and its historical P/E range is 12× to 20×, the company is trading near the low end of the range. If the broad market is trading at 17×, then the target company is also trading at a discount to the overall market. If the company's earnings are growing at a faster rate than that of the overall market as defined by the S&P 500 (assuming the target company is a large cap stock), then you are getting faster-growing earnings and paying less per dollar of earnings than you would for the broad market. In addition, if the company's earnings growth rate is in excess of its P/E, its PEG ratio is less than 1.0, which is also favorable.

Other traditional valuation metrics include **price-to-book** and **price-to-sales** ratios. For companies within the retail industry, price-to-sales is a key ratio. For companies within the financial industry, comparing a company's price to its book value is an important step because financial companies tend to trade at some multiple of **book value**. In general, when financial companies are trading at less than 'book' they might be compelling buys, whereas when they begin trading at 1.5× to 2× book they are heading toward overvaluation. As with all industries, market leaders tend to trade at a premium vis-à-vis their peers. For example, Goldman Sachs, Inc. (GS) has traditionally traded at around 0.5× book higher than its competitors, a multiple largely justified by its superior management, trading prowess, and ability to avoid the major mistakes to which its peers have fallen prey. A company's strength within its industry must therefore be weighed when considering these financial metrics. There is a reason why a given company is number one in its industry. Investors are almost always better off buying the preeminent company in an industry rather than the second or third best competitor. Companies with dominant market shares—the so-called best-of-breeds—are well positioned to take advantage of their weaker brethren's challenges. In addition to possessing greater market share, a market leader can be the company with the greatest sales or profitability. Other competitive advantages include patents, trademarks, and brand identity.

**Return on equity (ROE)** is another consideration when measuring the financial strength of your investment targets. A company's return on equity is the amount of earnings per share divided by its equity per share. You should look for high and consistent ROE, preferably above 10%.

Finally, an often overlooked but vital financial criterion is that of balance-sheet strength. Most investors focus on a company's profit and loss (P&L) statement because this is where all the 'action' is. However, a company's balance-sheet strength, or lack thereof, often determines the company's ability to survive and possibly thrive during inevitable industry-specific or macroeconomic downturns—those twenty-five-year floods that happen every three to five years.

*Figure* **3.3 Chart of CVX Strong Balance Sheet Supporting Stock**

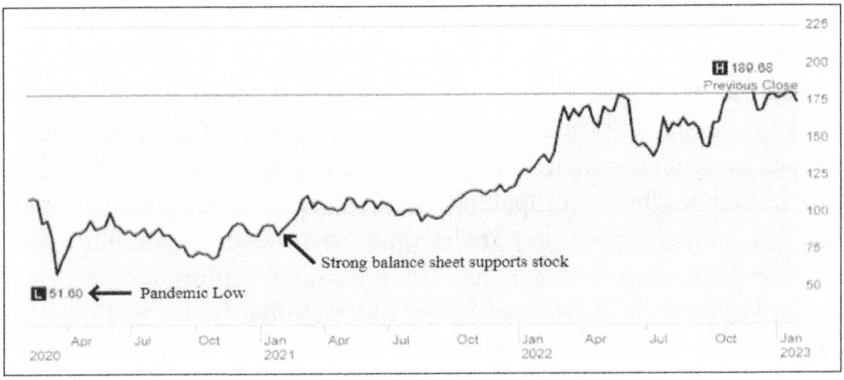

SOURCE: CHARLES SCHWAB

Examining Chevron Corp (CVX), the company faced collapsing oil prices multiple times, the price of oil dropping from over $100 a barrel in 2014 to under $30 in 2015. During the height of the pandemic, oil plunged yet again, briefly going negative in April, 2020. If Chevron had a weak balance sheet—if it were highly leveraged with little to no cash on its books—then it would likely have been forced to cut its dividend as many other oil related companies did during both periods. To be sure, CVX did see its stock price decline during this time, however it continued to not only pay its dividend quarter after quarter, it raised its payout each year including in Feb 2023, approaching 40 straight years of dividend increases.

Compare this example with the dividend cuts made by its peers Schlumberger Limited (SLB), British Petroleum PLC (BP), and Occidental Petroleum Corp (OXY), not to mention countless second and third-tier companies in the industry which eliminated their dividends entirely if not went bankrupt. Why did these companies feel compelled to do what all companies loathe to do, cut their dividend? Predominantly due to their weak balance sheets. This is an important lesson when it comes to equity analysis and financial appraisal. When in doubt, invest in companies with rock-solid balance sheets; look for the industry leaders, the best-of-breed companies that will not be the ones to fail when the inevitable business and financial challenges arise. This focus on quality companies with solid balance sheets will, in and of itself, be a large source of risk reduction when it comes to portfolio construction.

Now that we are convinced that we have to look beyond the P&L to determine a viable investment candidate, what are some basic balance sheet items that can give us confidence or pause? Just as individual consumers who are leveraged up with mortgages, car loans, and credit card debt are at risk for a single bad financial event putting them over the edge, so too are companies with weak balance sheets just a recession or a delayed product launch away from financial disaster. What are some metrics that we can examine to see whether a company is close to a precipice or standing on solid ground?

The balance sheet summarizes a company's assets, liabilities, and shareholders' equity. Basic balance-sheet considerations include the **current ratio**, which is the current assets divided by current liabilities. While acceptable current ratios vary industry by industry, you should generally seek companies with ratios in the 1.5 to 2.0 range. Too low a ratio means that the company may have challenges meeting its short-term obligations whereas a ratio which is too high may mean the company is not using its current assets efficiently. The **working capital** ratio looks at current assets minus current liabilities. This figure will help you determine whether a company is able to meet its near-term obligations. A higher number is preferable, which makes intuitive sense. **Leverage** is a key measure of a company's capital structure. Does a company rely solely on its own equity to finance its assets (in other words, is it debt free?), or does it also employ debt? If the latter, how much debt is on the company's books? By dividing long-term debt by the company's total equity, you can determine a basic level of leverage. While some level of leverage can help to improve a company's return on equity (assuming the capital is deployed in a way that the return on the capital exceeds the cost of the capital), a company with too much leverage puts itself at risk of not being able to meet its obligations if its operations suffer an unexpected disruption. Unlike the profit and loss statement, the balance sheet can seem complex and murky, thus most novice investors avoid balance-sheet analysis entirely. While you do not have to read every footnote of the quarterly 10-Q, by focusing on basic and understandable measures, you will increase the probability that the company you invest in will continue to send you checks for years to come as their asset-and-liability house will be in order, thus securing both their own and your financial futures.

## The Big Picture

Macroeconomic analysis—using economic indicators such as GDP rates, inflation levels, interest rates, and unemployment rates—is considered by many fundamental investors to be the least important consideration when making long-term stock selections. No one can consistently forecast major economic barometers. As the old saying goes, economists have predicted nine of the last five recessions. Even if you dedicated your entire professional life to studying, understanding, and predicting various economic criteria, you would be wrong most of the time when the news was actually released (to be later revised in most cases). Even if you manage to get a data point correct from time to time, accurately predicting both the timing and magnitude of the event in question (e.g., the unfolding of a recession within a certain time period) creates additional challenges. Further, and more to the point as an investor, you must also accurately predict the market's reaction to such events. Consistently doing so in such a way that the undertaking adds value to your portfolio is a near impossibility. While it is true that certain sectors tend to outperform in a recession (health care, consumer staples), the drivers for a given economic cycle tend to differ each time, and the economy has a way of surprising even the smartest academics, let alone investors. Less than 5% of your investing-related time, if any time at all, should be dedicated to macroeconomic considerations. Warren Buffett is quoted as saying he spends around 5 minutes per year on economic forecasting which is "probably 5 minutes too much." You get the point.

If you are going to pick one macroeconomic variable to focus on it would interest rates, as higher rates tend to have a negative impact on stock valuations ("gravity" as Buffett describes it), especially for growth companies as investors experienced in 2022 when rates finally rose after a decade of being largely dormant (and historically low). It is easy in retrospect to say interest rates were going to rise, but in reality, many smart economists had been predicting the rise in rates for years. Were you to invest based on these predictions - and focus exclusively on value stocks (which tend to do better in a rising rate environment) rather than also having some exposure to growth stocks, you would have missed one of the greatest periods of growth stock outperformance in history (2020 – 2021, driven in part of course by something entirely unpredicted: the pandemic). As always, focus on best-of-breed companies whether value or growth.

## Technical Analysis – Bottom's Up

In general, the longer the holding period, the more company fundamentals matter, and the less technical variables are part of the equation. Conversely, the shorter the holding period, the more technical indicators matter, and the less fundamentals play a role. Do you have a ten-year time horizon for holding stock? If so, fundamental factors such as stock valuation and competitive position within an industry should dominate the analysis. Looking to buy or sell an equity option to expire within a few days? Then fundamentals are of little consideration and technical analysis is paramount.

**Figure 3.4 Fundamental Versus Technical Analysis
Time Frame Considerations**

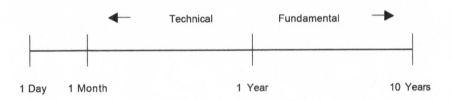

Entire books have been written on technical analysis, so I would recommend picking up one of the better tomes if you have a penchant for reading this sort of thing. Technical analysis, by and large, consists of looking at charts and retroactively justifying the movement in a stock's price. This approach pays no consideration to what is happening with a given company on an elemental level. If a chart shows an upward trend and a stock breaks above a given resistance level, a technical analyst might well recommend the stock *after* it has gone up, regardless of whether the fundamentals have changed during the interim. Technical analysis is principally beneficial when used in conjunction with fundamental analysis to determine whether a stock has created what is called a 'bottom.' Value investors are often looking for that otherwise solid company which has fallen on hard times; value investors tend to be early. The time that it will take to turn around the situation in question is often underestimated. Therefore, it can be helpful to look at a chart to see if the company's stock price has stabilized before taking a position as noted in Figure 3.5.

**Figure 3.5 Charting a Stock Hitting a Bottom**

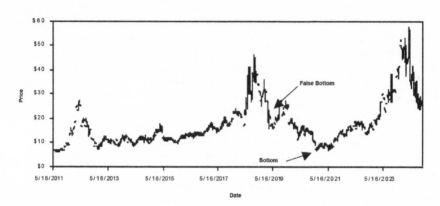

Another technical tool that can be helpful, especially when the use of options is part of your portfolio construction, is the volatility indicator VIX. VIX measures the implied volatility of the S&P 500 over thirty days.

Individual stocks also have their own historical and implied volatility measures. Given the relationship between high volatility levels and low stock or market prices, a high VIX or individual stock volatility reading can be a useful piece of information in validating a favorable entry point.

Trading volumes as well as insider trading (when executives of the company either buy or sell their own company's stock) are two other technical indicators that can provide insight as to whether a stock has formed a base. Often sell-offs in a given stock or the market as a whole are accompanied by very large volumes—panic selling by investors who 'cannot take it anymore,' who must sell because they are getting margin calls from their brokers, or who need to raise money to pay their bills. Sales often beget sales for those in a position of weakness. Look at the average daily trading volumes for a given stock. A new low with a larger-than-average volume can be a positive sign that the selling has been exhausted and a bottom is being created. Furthermore, smart company directors and senior executives will often sell large blocks of stock near the tops and will put their own money to work during low points. While not a definitive indicator in and of itself, these technical indicators can provide clues as to future stock behavior.

33

## *Figure* 3.6 Volume and Price Overlay

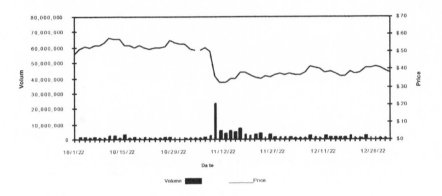

As depicted in Figure 3.6, in early November 2022, Company X stock fell approximately 20% with trading volume spiking to over 27 million shares on a single day. In the the days leading up to the plunge, the average daily volume level for Company X was around three million shares. This is a common scenario in which a huge volume increase accompanies a large price decline.

Similarly, you can examine charts to see where a stock or **exchange traded fund (ETF)** has traded over a certain time period. Often when a security has dropped in price, it is tempting to get in on the rationale that, if the stock has dropped 20%, it must now be of compelling value. Without a longer-term price appreciation perspective, however, one can lose sight of the fact that the security may have previously increased several hundred percentage points, and thus a 20% drop off its recent highs represents only a small portion of the total decline potential inherent in the security, based on the longer-term run-up as depicted in the figures below.

*Figure* **3.7 Short-Term Perspective on Stock Decline**

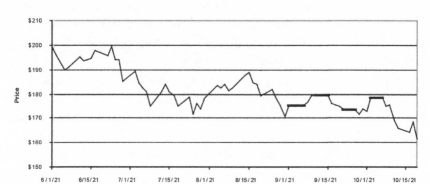

*Figure* **3.8 Long-Term Perspective to Assess Stock Decline**

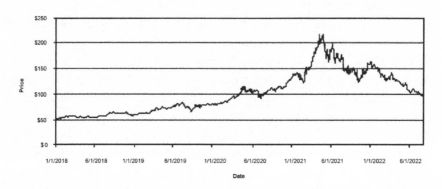

The fact is, stocks can drop by 20% repeatedly. A $50 stock dropping 20% goes to $40. A 20% decline from there puts the stock at $32. Another 20% slump puts the stock at $25.60. Ask someone how much a stock that has dropped 20% three times has declined in total and the typical answer will be 60%, or for the more sophisticated, "more than 60% given the math of compounding." Wrong both times. The stock has not even declined 50% yet. The math gets even uglier. Another 20% drop puts the stock at $20.48, and a fifth decline of 20% puts the stock at $16.38. That is five 20% drops and the stock is 'only' down 67% door-to-door. Another 20% drop puts the stock at $13.10

and down a little over 73%. That means a whopping incremental 20% plummet only decreased the total loss by a little over 6% on an absolute basis. (When you look at the math behind making up for losses, you will quickly see that being down 70% versus being down 60% is a much larger difference than it appears).

Therefore, charts can put into perspective how much stocks have run up and how much they can fall. When you are in the heat of the stock market day and you see a stock or sector 'crack' 20% and are tempted to jump on this opportunity, check a longer-term chart to put the near-term price movements into a longer-term perspective. Also be sure to employ the three-day rule which is to wait at least three trading days from the time you consider an idea to actually pulling the trigger. More times than not the stock has more room to fall before finding a bottom, and if you can't wait three days before putting your hard-earned money into long-term assets you may want to rethink your approach to investing.

In summary, technical analysis has a limited place in stock selection, thus, as with macroeconomic analysis, it should consume less than 10% of your total money-management-related time if your time horizon is a year or longer, and perhaps 10% to 20% of your time if you are predominantly a trader rather than an investor. And you can certainly outperform the market with zero technical analysis incorporated into your stock selection process. There are few if any purely technical analysts, or chartists, who consistently outperform the market year after year, so use technical analysis as a 'validator' of your fundamental analysis and focus your time and energy on areas where true value can be added to your portfolio.

## Demographics

Demographic analysis is the practice of looking at long-term trends in society and the economy at large to identify industries or companies that will benefit from broad shifts in such things as migration, and the ratio between urban and suburban dwellers. One example would be the aging of America. Statistics about the number of baby boomers entering retirement, for example, might support an investment in health care companies that would benefit from increased prescription drug use.

## *Industry Analysis*

Industry analysis is the next criterion to use when building a high-quality portfolio. Now we are starting to get into areas beyond fundamental/valuation analysis that truly merit the majority of our time and attention as investors. Even for those who focus on individual stock selection as opposed to building a portfolio of ETFs, industry analysis is essential for increasing the probability that they are at least playing in the right field.

**Figure 3.9 Industry Sectors**

1. **Information Technology**
2. **Health Care**
3. **Financials**
4. **Consumer Discretionary**
5. **Communication Services**
6. **Industrials**
7. **Consumer Staples**
8. **Energy**
9. **Utilities**
10. **Real Estate**
11. **Materials**

SOURCE: MORGAN STANLEY CAPITAL
INTERNATIONAL AND STANDARD & POOR'S

The above sectors can be broken down in more detail. For example, within the financial grouping, you have brokerage, mortgage, thrift, insurance, REITs, regional banking, and the like.

What should you look for in industry analysis? One simple but effective framework is known as the Five Forces. This approach analyzes: (1) competition within the industry, (2) potential for new entrants, (3) power of suppliers, (4) power of customers, and (5) threat of substitute products. Add to this technological change that makes a given offering or process obsolete (the disruption principle).

For competition, examine how many competitors there are within the industry. How large are they? Are they well financed? Is the industry fragmented (e.g., laundry, with hundreds or thousands of competitors) or concentrated (such as the aerospace industry with its small number of players)? Is this an industry that requires a significant amount of capital to enter, or are barriers to entry quite low?

Other considerations include geographic area. Is the industry local in nature? National? Global? What is the industry size? What are the trends? What is the outlook? How is the regulatory environment?

Demographic and psychographic attributes of the industry and its customers are also important. Demographic information includes population and household size, median income, age, sex, race; psychographic considerations include lifestyle information, tastes, and buying habits.

Most people have other full-time jobs, families to look after, and hobbies to enjoy. Taking the time to become an expert in so many areas is difficult if not impossible. Thus, fundamental company analysis is where the vast majority of investing research time should be dedicated. At the end of the day, it is how much a company earns—and how much you paid for those earnings—that largely determines investing success.

Key Takeaways:

- Look beyond stock price to valuation metrics such as P/E and PEG ratios so see if a stock is an attractive investment candidate.
- When market P/E ratios are lower, future returns tend to be higher. Use this to your advantage for incremental investments.
- Focus your investments on securities that are both good companies and good stocks.
- Don't ignore a company's balance sheet when considering investment opportunities – especially for dividend paying companies.
- Technical analysis can help investors see the bigger picture when considering entry points for investments.
- It is good to be familiar with the various industry designations, but focus on high quality, financially sound companies independent of industry placement.

# CHAPTER 4

## KEEPING YOUR OPTIONS OPEN

The focus of this chapter is on how to use options to generate income, enhance returns, and provide downside protection. Options can be complex and confusing, if not outright intimidating. Many people think of derivatives in general or options in particular as risky. To be sure, any vehicle can be a source of danger depending on how it is used. A knife in the hands of an ill intended robber is dangerous; a blade in the palm of a talented surgeon can be lifesaving. The purpose of this chapter is to provide you the tools to use options in conjunction with quality dividend-paying companies to your financial advantage.

An option is a derivative, which is simply a fancy term for the fact that the option's movement in price is a function of an underlying security, be it a stock, ETF, index, or other investment vehicle. The easiest and best way to think about options is to compare them to insurance. When you buy fire insurance, for example, you sign a contract (the policy) and pay money (the insurance premium) in order to be protected against the occurrence of a fire for a specified period of time (the duration of the contract). If the event does occur prior to the expiration of the contract period, then you receive whatever your contract calls for (e.g., the replacement cost of your house).

The insurance company hopes the event you are protecting yourself against never occurs. If your house does not burn down, the insurance company keeps the entire premium you paid without making any payments itself, an outcome that adds to the company's profits. Of course, accidents do occur, and insurance policies are paid out periodically. The insurance company's goal is to write (AKA sell) enough policies and price them in such a way that after collecting all the premiums and paying out all the claims—and paying operating costs—it ends up with a big profit.

Let's apply this analogy to options. Say you are planning to buy a house in the next year. You anticipate the house will cost $1,000,000. You intend to borrow 75% of the cost, thus you need $250,000 as a down payment. You own 1,000 shares of Company X, which currently trades for $270 per share. For tax or other reasons you do not want to sell your shares today—perhaps you think Company X's stock will go up in the coming months or maybe you want to wait until your holding period exceeds one year so that you are subject to capital rather than income gains. However, this is your sole source of funds for the down payment on that home and you want to be sure that you have at least $250,000 when it comes time to purchase the house. How do you ensure if not insure this outcome? You can buy stock insurance; in this case you can buy a **put option**, which gives you the right, but not the obligation, to sell a stock at a given price during a specified period. For those speculating on price appreciation, a **call option** gives you the right to buy a stock at a given price for a certain time period.

Back to our soon-to-be homeowner. In this case you might buy Company X insurance to be sure you will receive at least $250 per share for your stock during the course of the contract. In other words, you would buy—pay a premium for—a put option that would give you the right, *no matter what happens with Company X's stock price,* to sell the stock for a fixed price while the contract is in effect. Were the company to go bankrupt and the stock to fall to zero, you have locked in a preset sales price of $250 per share. In order to buy 1,000 shares' worth of protection, the put buyer would need to purchase ten contracts, as each option contract represents 100 shares of the underlying security. For an option priced at $3.50 per contract, you would be fully covered by paying $3,500 (10 contracts X 100 shares per contract X $3.50 per share = $3,500 of premium paid). By entering into such a put option contract, a Company X investor is certain to have at least $250,000 of stock when it comes time to make the down payment. Whether this insurance is worth it, whether the contract is of good value, is up to the buyer of the insurance.

As with stock, options have a **bid price** and an **ask price**, the former being the price at which an option can be sold and the latter the price at which the option can be bought. The difference, or delta, between the bid and ask is the **spread**. You will often also see the last trade listed on a quote screen. This is simply the price at which the most recent trade was made. This may differ substantially from bid/ask quotes for relatively illiquid options. (For portfolio valuation purposes, you should use a mid-point between bid/ask rather than the last trade price). A typical option might be trading at $0.80 by $0.90, meaning that you could sell the option for $0.80 per contract and buy the option for $0.90 per contract. Often you will see such wide spreads in options—sometimes 30% or more—whereas highly liquid securities might trade at a .01% spread. In options trading in general, and particularly in cases where liquidity is low, it is vital that orders be placed on a **limit order** rather than a **market order** basis. If you are not **filled** at your initial limit price, the spread will often narrow, at which point you can adjust your limit order to see if you will get filled there. As with most things in life, you won't get anything unless you ask!

When stocks traded in fractions, options premiums traded in one-eighths. The introduction of decimal pricing helped to narrow spreads in options, which are inherently less efficient in terms of bid/ask spreads than equities due in part to their lower liquidity.

*Figure* **4.1 Spreads Associated with Option Increments**

| Options Trading In | Bid | Ask | Spread | % Spread |
|---|---|---|---|---|
| Dimes | $0.50 | $0.60 | $0.10 | 20% |
| Nickels | $0.50 | $0.55 | $0.05 | 10% |
| Pennies | $0.50 | $0.51 | $0.01 | 2% |

As options began to trade in smaller units, the spread percentages decreased dramatically, increasing options' market efficiency and improving their cost effectiveness.

The stated price per share at which the buyer can purchase (in the case of a call) or sell (in the case of a put) a given stock is called the **strike price**. Typically strike prices are spaced in either 1, 2.5, or 5-point increments. For example, a stock trading at $38 per share may have options with strike prices of $32.50, $35, $37.50, $40, $42.50, and so on.

The date on which the contract ends is called the **expiration date**. Most options expire on the Saturday following the third Friday of each month, with trading ending at close of day that Friday. There are important exceptions, however, as noted below. Some securities have options that expire each month, while others have option expiration dates that are quarterly. You can also buy or sell an option mid-cycle, as options are traded on all market days. This means that you can establish virtually limitless positions that take into consideration intra-month events such as earnings announcements. Certain widely traded options, such as the ones that trade on the very popular SPYs, have what are called 'weeklies,' or options that expire every week rather than every month. There are even 'dailies' for those so inclined.

There are two main types of expiration, **American-style** and **European-style**. American-style options can be exercised at any time by their owners, while European-style options can only be exercised on their expiration dates. This is an important consideration for options that become in-the-money prior to expiration and can be assigned prematurely (in the case of American-style). Furthermore, most European-style options are **cash-settled based**, meaning the owner of the option gets credited cash (or is debited) in the amount equal to the difference between the index's closing price and the strike price of the option rather than receiving any securities. The owner of an American-style option, however, must buy or sell the stock depending on whether he is a holder of puts or calls, and then buy/sell the newly acquired underlying security in order to profit accordingly. Most individual stock equity options, as well as those available on ETFs (e.g., SPY, which is the S&P 500; QQQ, which is the NASDAQ 100; or DIA, which is the Dow Jones Industrial Average) trade American-style through the end of trading on the third Friday of each month. Most index options (e.g., SPX, NDX), however, trade European-style and stop trading at the end of the day on the Thursday before the third Friday of each month.

It is important to note that the price for which the European-style options settle—or the **settlement price**—is determined on the Friday morning following the end of trading on Thursday and may differ dramatically from the final price the day before. This is an important consideration when deciding whether to close out options prior to expiration. In effect, you enter a blackout period for about sixteen hours, with events occurring during this period that could affect your pocketbook though you are unable to manage the position—not just because market hours are over, but because it is 'game over' for the particular option (but the score is still being tallied).

Remember, however, that just because a European-style option cannot be exercised prior to expiration does not mean it cannot be traded prior to expiration. It can be traded any time the market for options is open, with European-style options often trading until 4:15 P.M. EST rather than 4:00 P.M., when most equity markets close for business. As a good rule of thumb, if you are short index options that are within 2% of being in-the-money, it is best to close them out before the blackout period between Thursday's close and Friday's open. While, statistically speaking, it will not happen often, all it takes is one 3%+ overnight move to wipe out all the gains you made from letting your near-the-money options expire. It takes a lot of nickel gains to make up for one multi-dollar loss, and the period around options expiration is not called the witching hour for nothing; the third Thursday and Friday of each month tend to be some of the most volatile periods. So do the smart thing and buy back out-of-the-money and about-to-expire European-style index options for a nickel and change. You will be glad you did on the one morning a year you wake up to some dramatic event that causes the market to open at a materially different price than the previous session's close. Unless you are a full time, professional options trader, you should focus on American-style options and generally stay clear of European-style.

The ability to buy and sell options with varying expiration dates at varying strike prices allows the options trader to fine-tune his hedging, trading, or speculating strategies. Note also that there is limited **counterparty risk** in trading options, meaning the person or institution with whom you have entered into the transaction will not fail to fulfill their contractual obligation. In general, when agreements involve only two parties, then counterparty risk is at its greatest; when a well-established and financially sound intermediary is involved, counterparty risk is mitigated. In the case of listed derivatives, the exchange's clearinghouse is the counterparty to each option sale or purchase, eliminating the possibility that you will be unable to sell the stock on which you have purchased put options.

## OPTIONS LEVELS AND QUALIFICATIONS

There are four different levels of options trading. A broker determines the level for which an investor qualifies depending on the nature of the account as well as variables that include the investor's lifetime trading experience, **net worth**, income, number of trades made per year, and average trade size. For qualified accounts (IRAs, etc.), the types of options you can trade are limited by law, regardless of how much experience you have or how large the account is. These limits are meant to protect investors from taking on too much risk in their retirement accounts. The following represents the various options levels and what types of trades can be conducted given the level of options-trading authorization:

**Level 0:**  This level allows for covered options and protective options, long stock/short calls (covered calls), long stock/long puts (protective puts), short stock/short puts (covered puts), and short stock/long calls (protective calls).

**Level 1:**  This level allows all of the level 0 transactions plus long options, long puts and calls, long straddles, long combos, long strangles, and cash-secured equity put-writing.

**Level 2:**  This level includes all transactions in levels 0 and 1 plus spreads, credit and debit spreads, diagonal call and put spreads, and ratio spreads.

**Level 3:**  This level includes all transactions in levels 0 to 2 plus uncovered options, uncovered puts and calls, short straddles, short strangles, and short combos.

It is important to know the level for which you qualify and the types of options that you can trade. Note that some firms use the scale 0 to 3 while others use 1 to 4. Even for investors who otherwise qualify, brokerage firms often require an initial minimum equity account value of $25,000 or more for the sale of options. Note that some of the more aggressive techniques detailed in this book (e.g., naked calls) are only available to those who qualify for the highest level of options trading. Be sure to consult your broker or financial institution to determine the tools you can use in your trading program.

## TRADING OPTIONS

**Option chains** are listed on the **CBOE** (Chicago Board Options Exchange) and other popular websites, where the following information is provided: underlying security ticker symbol, strike price, expiration date, and type of option (call or put).

In looking up option quotes, you will see, as with stocks, the **volume** of contracts traded. You will also see a term called **open interest**, which is the total number of contracts not yet exercised or expired and which should not be confused with volume. Open interest gives you a sense of the liquidity associated with a given option. A low or zero open interest position generally means that there is little activity in the option. Spreads for such options are generally large, and thus you should place limit orders rather than market orders so that prices received are not surprisingly different from published bid/ask spreads. That said, when calculating your potential return from a buy write, for example, only the amount you receive for selling the call matters in determining if the return potential is favorable. Even if after selling the option you show a loss by virtue of the option being priced at the ask post-sale, eventually the option price will come in and you will capture the entire profit potential associated with the price you received for your option sale. In addition, large trading volume relative to open interest is an indication of high activity and interest in the company on which the options are being traded.

As discussed above, the buyer of an option pays a premium to the seller of the option. This premium has three components: the **total premium**, the **intrinsic value premium**, and the **time value premium**. Let's examine each. The total premium is just what the name implies: it is the amount paid for the option contract. The **intrinsic value** is the amount by which an option is **in-the-money (ITM)**. Let's say you buy a put option for $2.50 per contract, giving you the right to sell ABC stock at $25 per share (the strike price). At the time you buy this put, ABC is selling for $24 per share. Under this put scenario, the option is in-the-money, thus the intrinsic value of the option is $1, which is the strike price minus the share price. Since the total premium is made up of the intrinsic value and the time premium, the remaining $1.50 premium must be time premium. Only when options are in-the-money do they have intrinsic value. Options that are sold **out-of-the-money (OTM)** have no intrinsic value, only time value. In the example above, if ABC were selling for $26 per share when you bought the $25 put, the cost of the put would have been perhaps $0.80, the entire premium being time value.

*Figure* **4.2 Time Value Versus Intrinsic Value for Puts**

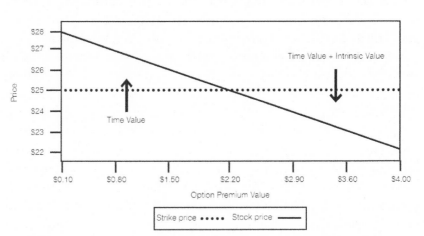

In basic terms, call option buyers want the underlying stock to go up; this is a bullish or 'long' bet. Conversely, put buyers want the price of the underlying security to go down in order to profit from the position. This is a 'short' or bearish bet. When you buy an option contract you are **buying to open**. If you sell this contract, you are **selling to close**. If you sell the option short instead of buying a put or call long, you are **selling to open**. For example, if ABC is trading at $28 per share and you want to own 1,000 shares of the stock, but only at a lower price, you may sell ten contracts of $27.50 puts to open. If the put option price is $1.20 of premium per contract, you will receive $1,200. If the underlying stock price goes up and the short put contracts begin to lose value, you might choose to **buy to close** the contracts, thus completing the transaction (selling high, buying low). Alternately, you can wait until expiration date to have the option expire worthless if the stock is trading above the strike price in the case of holding a put short.

*Figure* 4.3 Option Transactions

| | | |
|---|---|---|
| **Put** | Buy Put to Open<br><br>Sell Put to Close | Sell Put to Open<br><br>Buy Put to Close |
| **Call** | Buy Call to Open<br><br>Sell Call to Close | Sell Call to Open<br><br>Buy Call to Close |

## Selling Options

Selling options can be confusing at first since selling a put to open seems like a double negative. If you are getting confused, place yourself in the position of the option buyer. In buying a put, you want the stock to drop in order to profit. If you are the seller of the put, you want the opposite to occur, the stock price to go up. Using the insurance example, the seller of the option has in effect sold insurance to the buyer of the option, the seller betting that the event being protected against (in this case the stock price falling below the strike price) never occurs. Note that some put sellers do want to get assigned (to own the stock at a lower price) thus not all put sellers want the underlying stock to go up.

Rather than buying an option to close that you originally sold to open, you might also let an option contract expire if the stock price is above the strike price (in the case of a put) or below the strike price (in the case of a call). Put another way, if an option is out-of-the-money at the time of expiration, you do not need to close out the contract; rather, you can simply let it expire worthless and save the commission dollars and the nickel or dime per share you will need to pay when OTM about-to-expire options are trading at $0 × $0.05 or $0.10.

If an option is in-the-money—the stock price is below the strike price in the case of a put or above the strike price in the case of a call—you might choose to become **exercised**, or **assigned**, which means you are required to buy the stock if you have sold puts or sell the stock if you are short covered calls (if you are short naked calls, you become short the stock upon expiration, which is the mirror image of being required to buy the stock long if your short puts become assigned). Any option that is in-the-money $0.01 or more at the time of expiration will be subject to being exercised.

Note that whether you are long or short an option, you do not have to get assigned—or exercise the option—if it is in-the-money. You can always close out the transaction prior to expiration without ever owning the underlying security as noted in Figure 4.4. For example, if you bought ABC $25 calls long for $0.75 per contract and the stock is trading at $28 per share just prior to expiration, you can sell the calls at a profit that will be equivalent to your exercising the option and selling the stock at the then market price. In the case of selling the option, its value would be approximately $3.10 just prior to expiration ($3 of intrinsic value and a few pennies of time value). If, instead of selling the call option in the secondary market for $3.10, you exercised the option, you would buy the stock at $25 per share and either hold the shares or immediately sell the stock at $28 per share (the then market price), which would again yield an approximate $3 per-share profit. Note that options can be assigned prior to the expiration date, so if you do not want to buy/sell the stock when an option is ITM, you may want to close the position to avoid getting prematurely assigned.

## Rolling Options

In addition to either closing out your option contract prior to expiration or exercising it upon expiration, another alternative is to **roll** your

*Figure* 4.4 **Closing an ITM Option Contract**

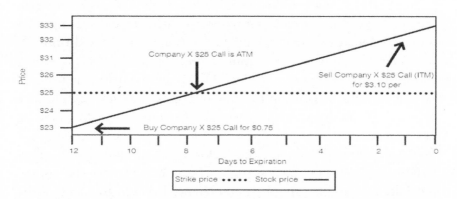

option to a later-dated expiration period. Rolling an option involves buying the about-to-expire option to close and concurrently selling to open a later-dated option either at the same strike price (a straight time roll) or a different strike price (to **roll up and out**). This is an advanced technique that can optimize the benefits associated with receiving time premium. For example, if you have sold an OTM $27.50 put and the stock price has dropped to $26.50, the option price will be trading for a little over $1 just prior to expiration. Rather than being assigned or permanently closing out the position, you might choose to buy back the put and roll it out to a later-dated expiration date, receiving what is called a **delta premium**. You might also hear the term **credit spread**, which represents the net gain from proceeds received by way of selling an option with a higher price less the money spent in concurrently buying back the original option at a lower price. While the difference is subtle, we are differentiating between the common trading practice of simultaneously buying/selling two options with different strike prices for a net credit and the technique of closing one option out and selling a later-dated option to take its place. The latter, which we are terming the delta premium, is simply the difference between the price of the about-to-expire option premium you are buying to close and the price of the option premium you are selling to open for the later-dated option. The goal is to buy the put back for $1.10, for example, and to sell a later-dated option for $1.50, gaining a net credit to your account of $0.40 per share, which represents the thirty or sixty days of additional time premium. You would typically do this if you still felt bullish on the underlying stock but did not want to own it and thus chose not to get assigned.

On the call side, if you have bought a stock at $28 and sold the $30 calls for $1.50 of premium, the stock might close just below $30 at time of expiration. If you are hesitant on the stock or if the market is behaving bearishly, you could roll down rather than rolling out or up by selling the ITM $27.50s for the most significant protection (remember, you have already collected $1.50 premium, so your effective purchase price has been lowered to $26.50, thus even selling the $27.50s at this time allows for profits on the position even though your stock purchase price was $28 per share). Clearly, your upside potential is limited here, but you are giving yourself some solid downside safety. The middle-of-the-road tactic would be to sell the later dated $30 strike price calls. If, however, you are feeling bullish on the stock you can roll the options up and out by selling the $32.50s, which will offer you the least amount of premium but the greatest amount of upside capital potential. When deciding what strike price to sell next, you are weighing the trade-offs of maximum gains/least protection associated with a higher strike price versus lower gains/maximum protection that the ATM or ITM calls afford you.

There will also be times when the call you sold earlier is trading for pennies several weeks before expiration. If you sold a call for $1.00 per contract and it is now trading at $0.05 X $0.10 a week or more prior to expiration, you have already captured in excess of 80% of the total profit potential associated with this position. Rather than waiting until expiration to pick up the final nickel or two, consider rolling the option to a later-dated expiration period once you have captured 80% or more of the profit potential associated with the about-to-expire option. In waiting until expiration, you are giving up premium associated with options with later-dated expirations. Simply put, you have only a few pennies to gain from the option you currently hold short, whereas you may lose much more than that in waiting until expiration, the later-dated options declining from $1.80 to $1.35 for example during the two-week period you are waiting for your (negative) few cents to turn into zero.

## Covered and Naked Options

As we have learned, options can be either bought or sold. When you buy an option, you are **long** the option. As with selling equities short—borrowing shares you do not own in hopes of buying them back at a lower price—when your first transaction is to sell an option, you are short the option. A short option can either be **covered** or **naked**.

An example of the former would be a **covered call** option, also known as a **buy write** as depicted in Figure 4.5. This occurs when you own stock long and sell, or **write**, calls against that long stock. If no long equity position existed, the call would be naked rather than covered. In this case you buy a stock long for $27 and sell $27.50 calls for $0.80 per contract. The chart shows various outcomes depending on the stock price at the time of expiration, along with the opportunity cost for having sold the calls should the stock close higher than the strike price plus premium earned.

*Figure 4.5* Covered Call Scenarios

| Closing Price at Expiration | Outcome | Total Position Profit | Profit Source | Opportunity Cost (of Selling Stock Instead of Options) |
|---|---|---|---|---|
| $27.00 | Option expires worthless. | $0.80 | Full premium from option sale | $0.00 |
| $27.50 | Option expires worthless. | $1.30 | Full premium from option sale + $0.50 capital gains | $0.00 |
| $28.00 | Option is exercised. Forced to Sell Stock. | $1.30 | $0.8 0 + $2 7.50 - $27 | $0.00 |
| $28.50 | Option is exercised. Forced to Sell Stock. | $1.30 | $0.8 0 + $2 7.50 - $27 | $0.20 |
| $29.00 | Option is exercised. Forced to Sell Stock. | $1.30 | $0.8 0 + $2 7.50 - $27 | $0.70 |
| $29.50 | Option is exercised. Forced to Sell Stock. | $1.30 | $0.8 0 + $2 7.50 - $27 | $1.20 |

Covered calls limit your profit potential but provide some down-side protection. Were the stock to close sharply down, you would still benefit from the full premium of the option sale. However, if the stock were to close above the strike, your upside is limited to the premium you receive from the sale of the option, plus the strike price (the price at which you sold the stock to the option buyer) less the original stock purchase price. If the stock were to close above the strike and you had not sold options, your upside via capital gains would be unlimited.

Figure 4.6 demonstrates how covered calls work by examining a $50,000 portfolio. At its starting point, your portfolio shows $50,000 of cash and no other positions. In order to get some equity exposure, you buy 1,000 shares of broad-based ETF X trading at $49 per share. Now your portfolio shows a long position of 1,000 shares of ETF X at $49 per share for a total value of $49,000, plus $1,000 of cash. In order to generate income and provide some hedging, you sell short 10 OTM calls, specifically the $50 strike price calls for $2.30 of premium per share. What does your portfolio look like now? After the sale of the short calls, $2,300 of cash is deposited immediately into your account so that your cash balance is now $3,300. There is also an offsetting debit to the account, specifically a short position in the amount of ($2,300). This short position with a negative balance is just like any other position in your account. It can gain in value by becoming less negative or drop in value by becoming more negative.

*Figure* 4.6 Transaction Impacts on Positions

|  | Step 1 | Step 2 | Step 3 |
|---|---|---|---|
| **Action:** | Start Portfolio | Buy ETF | Short OTM Calls |
| **Positions:** | $50,000 Cash | $49,000 ETF<br>$1,000 Cash | $49,000 ETF<br>$3,300 Cash<br>($2,300) Short Calls on ETF |
| **Total Portfolio Value:** | $50,000 | $50,000 | $50,000 |

Three possible outcomes exist from this position: ETF X stays flat, ETF X decreases in price, or ETF X increases in price above $50 per share. Let's examine each scenario. If the ETF price is still $49 per share at the time of expiration, then the short position will be worth $0 (up from -$2,300). At this point you can elect to sell additional option premium via later-dated options or hold the position unhedged if you feel its capital gains prospects are sound. If the ETF price is below $49 per share at the time of expiration, you have still made $2,300 from selling the short call and you simply have an unrealized capital loss on the equity position itself. However, if the ETF is trading above $46.70 per share, you are still ahead on the total position as the $2.30 per share collected reduces your break-even point to $46.70, and, in any case, you are better off for having sold the calls. Finally, the stock price could be above $50 per share at the time of expiration. In this case, unless you close out (buy back) the option prior to expiration, your stock will be sold, or assigned, and you will have gained $1 per share, or $1,000 on your equity, in addition to the $2.30 per share for the covered calls.

In summary, the sale of calls on long positions in your portfolio is a conservative way to generate income and provide some downside protection. This strategy works particularly well for volatile positions that have recently had a big run-up and from which you are considering taking profits. If you want to own a stock for the long term and think it has considerable additional upside potential, you should not sell covered calls because you risk missing those future gains if you are forced to sell the stock. At a minimum in this scenario, you should only **hedge** part of the position (e.g., sell only five call contracts representing 500 shares if you own 1,000 shares of the stock).

As summarized in Figure 4.7, options provide flexibility, precision, and predictability; you can choose exact strike prices and expiration dates. You can elect to hedge a position in its entirety, or in any percentage thereof (e.g., if you own 1,000 shares of a given stock, you can sell a single call to hedge 10% of the position, two calls to hedge 20%, or any number of calls up to ten, which will make the long position fully covered). To focus on growth, buy growth stocks and sell few or no calls. To maximize income and downside protection, buy quality dividend-paying stocks and sell options that are very close to the money. You can focus on capital preservation and income by selling at-the-money calls on part of the position, and on capital gains by selling OTM calls on the remaining number of shares. While you cannot predict nor control future stock price movements, you can know with certainty the outcome of various options scenarios based on closing equity prices.

*Figure* 4.7 **Covered Call Gain/Hedge Scenarios**

| Strike Price | | Expiration Date | | | | |
|---|---|---|---|---|---|---|
| | | May | June | July | August | September |
| **$42.50** | Premium Earned | **$2.00** | **$2.75** | **$3.35** | **$4.80** | **$5.75** |
| | Max Gain | $0.33 | $1.08 | $1.68 | $3.13 | $4.08 |
| | Max Gain % | 0.75% | 2.45% | 3.80% | 7.09% | 9.24% |
| | Effective Sale Price | $44.50 | $45.25 | $45.85 | $47.30 | $48.25 |
| | Effective Hedge | 4.53% | 6.23% | 7.58% | 10.87% | 13.02% |
| | | | | | | |
| **$45.00** | Premium Earned | **$0.45** | **$1.32** | **$1.93** | **$3.50** | **$4.50** |
| | Max Gain | $1.28 | $2.15 | $2.76 | $4.33 | $5.33 |
| | Max Gain % | 2.90% | 4.87% | 6.25% | 9.80% | 12.07% |
| | Effective Sale Price | $45.45 | $46.32 | $46.93 | $48.50 | $49.50 |
| | Effective Hedge | 1.02% | 2.99% | 4.37% | 7.92% | 10.19% |
| | | | | | | |
| **$47.50** | Premium Earned | **$0.09** | **$0.52** | **$1.01** | **$2.43** | N/A |
| | Max Gain | $3.42 | $3.85 | $4.34 | $5.76 | |
| | Max Gain % | 7.74% | 8.72% | 9.83% | 13.04% | |
| | Effective Sale Price | $47.59 | $48.02 | $48.51 | $49.93 | |
| | Effective Hedge | 0.20% | 1.18% | 2.29% | 5.50% | |
| | | | | | | |
| **$50.00** | Premium Earned | **$0.03** | **$0.20** | **$0.48** | **$1.64** | **$2.60** |
| | Max Gain | $5.86 | $6.03 | $6.31 | $7.47 | $8.43 |
| | Max Gain % | 13.27% | 13.65% | 14.29% | 16.91% | 19.09% |
| | Effective Sale Price | $50.03 | $50.20 | $50.48 | $51.64 | $52.60 |
| | Effective Hedge | 0.07% | 0.45% | 1.09% | 3.71% | 5.89% |

## Shorting Calls

An uncovered short call sale is a different matter entirely. If you do not own Company X long and you sell the $27.50 calls, you have sold the calls naked. In this case—as with shorting a stock—your downside potential is unlimited, as Company X stock can go ever higher over time. However, selling calls short and naked can be considered a slightly less-risky version of shorting stock outright. How is that? Simple. Let's say two traders think Company X's stock price is headed south and want to make an aggressive bet on such an outcome. In Figure 4.8, Trader A sells short 1,000 shares of the stock outright at $27 per share. Trader B sells ten $27.50 call contracts (the equivalent of the same 1,000 shares) for $1.20 per contract. For every penny the stock goes up over $27 per share, Trader A begins to lose money. His losses start immediately as the stock price heads north. Trader B, on the other hand, does not start losing money until the stock gets to $28.70 per share, which equals the strike price plus the premium he has collected. That represents his break-even point. Only after the stock climbs 6.3% does Trader B begin to lose money.

### *Figure* 4.8 Profits from Shorting Stock Versus Shorting Calls

| Stock Price | Trader A Profits (Per share) | Trader B Profits (Per share) |
| --- | --- | --- |
| $0.00 | $27.00 | $1.20 |
| $25.50 | $1.50 | $1.20 |
| $26.00 | $1.00 | $1.20 |
| $26.50 | $0.50 | $1.20 |
| $27.00 | $0.00 Break Even | $1.20 |
| $27.50 | ($0.50) | $1.20 |
| $28.00 | ($1.00) | $0.70 |
| $28.50 | ($1.50) | $0.20 |
| $28.70 | ($1.70) | $0.00 Break Even |
| $29.00 | ($2.00) | ($0.30) |
| $29.50 | ($2.50) | ($0.80) |
| $30.00 | ($3.00) | ($1.30) |

But there is no such thing as a free lunch. Trader A can make up to $27 per share on the short equity position—the price at which he shorted the stock down to zero—whereas Trader B capped his gains at $1.20 per share, the amount he received for selling his naked calls. While these two short positions—the naked calls and the outright equity short—have similar characteristics and a common objective, the dynamics of each position differ.

## Shorting Puts

On the short put side, none other than Warren Buffett has used the sale of short puts to lower his effective purchase price, increase his returns via premiums collected, or both. Figure 4.9 demonstrates how it works. Let's say a stock is trading at $32 per share and you have a generally positive outlook on the company and its share price. However, you think there is a chance that the stock price will go down in the near term, and in any case, you would prefer owning the company at a lower entry point. To achieve this objective, you can sell out-of-the-money puts to lower your effective purchase price. If you sell the ten contracts of the $30 strike price puts and collect $1.50 per share, you have effectively lowered your purchase price to $28.50 per share.

**Figure 4.9 Short Put Profit Scenarios**

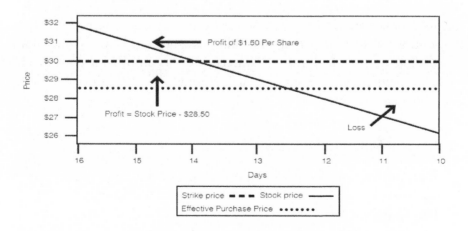

What are the possible outcomes under this scenario? The stock could close above $30 per share at time of expiration, in which case you profit from the maximum potential gain of $1.50 per contract X 100 shares, or $1,500 on ten contracts sold. If the stock price closes below $30 at time of expiration, then you are required to purchase the stock at $30 (assuming you do not roll the option). Since you have collected $1.50 per share of premium, any closing price above $28.50 represents profit. While a closing of the stock price below $28.50 would yield a near-term loss, the sale of a put on a stock that you otherwise wanted to own effectively lowers the purchase price and by mathematical definition increases the likelihood of superior returns over time. In this case, your effective purchase price was lowered by nearly 11%, from the then market price of $32 down to your effective entry price of $28.50.

What strike price puts should you sell? The more comfortable you are owning the stock, the closer to the money your short put sales can be. For example, if a stock is trading at $46 per share, you could sell the $45 strike price and collect a larger premium than if you sold the more conservative, farther out-of-the-money $42.50 strike price for less premium, the former yielding you perhaps $1.30 of premium whereas the latter might get you $0.65 per contract. If you would prefer not to own the stock but want to use the sale of short puts as a means to add profits to your portfolio, focus on selling puts that are farther out-of-the-money.

However, when you sell naked puts, you should assume for the purposes of entering the trade as well as for portfolio accounting and risk control considerations that you will be assigned on the put. Your sales of short puts are just a more conservative version of your traditional long equity position. Therefore, always employ the same discipline and fundamental research.

## Hedging Short Stock Positions

Short puts can also be used as a hedge against short equity positions, just as short calls can be used as a hedge against owning stock long. This strategy is referred to as a **sell write**. In this case, a trader enters into a short equity sale by borrowing shares, selling them, and buying them back at a lower price, thus profiting from the price difference. This is simply the mirror image of buying stocks long with the goal of selling them for a profit at a higher price. Whether you first buy low and then sell high, or first sell high and later buy low, the profit objective is the same. To hedge a short equity position, a trader might sell a put and collect the premium. The net effect is to cap the upside of the short position while providing a small hedge in case the stock goes against the trader. For example, if you have a bearish take on Stock X and want to short the stock but hedge your short position, you could sell short 1,000 of X at $27 while simultaneously selling ten contracts of the $25 puts. If you collect $1.50 of premium per share, your upside would be limited to $3.50 per share, which is the difference between the $27 price at which you sold the shares and the $25 strike price plus the $1.50 premium.

### *Figure* 4.10 Sell Write Profit Scenarios

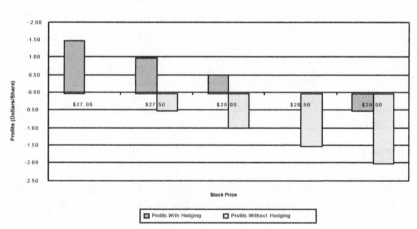

The graph in Figure 4.10 depicts the various profits attained from different stock price movements, given a short sale of stock. The stock is shorted at $27 a share. Assuming the position was not hedged with the short sale of puts, and if the stock price stayed at $27, profits would be zero. The investor would have borrowed shares, sold them at $27, and then bought them back at $27. If the stock price increased to $28, his loss would be $1 per share. If, instead of being naked short equity, the investor shorted the $25 puts to hedge his short equity position, he would have gained a premium of $1.50 a share. This premium acts as a cushion against losses on the short equity position in case the stock price rises. It also serves as a source of external discipline to take profits on a given position just like a short call against long stock. A sell write in effect 'forces' you to take profits on a short equity position when the underlying security has fallen to a predetermined level. Without this external source of discipline, you might hold on to your short position for too long and miss the window to take a profit should the market rebound. If the stock price were to stay at $27, the investor would have borrowed shares, sold them for $27, and then bought them back for $27. This time, however, because he shorted the puts, he would have gained that $1.50 premium. If the stock price were to increase to $28, the investor buys the shares back at $28 for a capital loss of $1. But with the cushion from the premium, his profits are at $0.50 ($1.50 premium − $1.00 capital loss).

If Stock X goes up, the sale of the short put provides a $1.50 per share cushion so that losses are only incurred once the stock goes above $28.50 per share. Losses would occur immediately for short sellers experiencing a rise in the share price without a short put hedge position.

**POWER TIP**
**Don't Get Stung—Let Options Be Your Pilot**

Most people hire personal trainers not because they are clueless about how to use weight machines, but because they need an external source of discipline to keep making smart physical choices. This function of a personal trainer offers real value. The sale of covered call options can be like your personal trainer—it impels disciplined sales at predetermined levels. When you might otherwise hold on to a stock for too long, the sale of an out-of-the-money call forces you to sell high, to take some profit chips off the table. For this reason alone, options can be a valuable tool in your trading and investing repertoire.

**POWER TIP**

**ATM is the Ultimate ATM**

When you own a stock long and have sold a short call against that long position, your best-case scenario is that the stock closes just at-the-money at time of expiration. For example, if you bought Company X for $32.20 per share and sold the $32.50 calls, a closing price of $32.49 or $32.50 would optimize the premium sold for the next-dated option. In this case, option ATM truly becomes a bank ATM machine.

| Stock Closing Price | Premium in $32.50 Calls |
|---|---|
| $31.50 | $0.40 |
| $32.00 | $0.75 |
| $32.50 | $1.00 |

These represent the bulk of the basic options trading techniques. There are others with fancy names like "Iron Condors" and "Butterfly Spreads," but the options strategies covered in this book are sufficient to take a myriad of positions that will provide upside profit and/or downside protection as dictated by a a given investing or trading strategy.

## VOLATILITY—THE VIX

There is an important concept within options called **volatility**, which can be defined as the amount by which an underlying security is expected to fluctuate in a given period. In layman's terms, some stocks move all over the place while others have a propensity to hold steady. Various factors contribute to this. How big a company is in terms of revenue and market capitalization can play an important role, larger companies generally being less volatile than their small-cap cousins. Older, more established companies (independent of market cap size) tend to see fewer swings in their stock price than newer listings because their earnings patterns have been demonstrated and there is less chance of a surprise in reported profits. The industry in which a company operates also plays a role in terms of options volatility, or "vol," as it is referred to on Wall Street. Stocks in high-growth industries and sectors that are less predictable in terms of product cycles (e.g., biotech) tend to be more volatile than industries like utilities, which typically have steadier, more foreseeable revenue streams.

The country of origin might also affect a stock option's volatility level. Stocks of companies based in more mature and stable economies like that of the United States are likely to be less volatile than those in emerging, potentially unstable countries. Finally, world events, be they economic, social, or political, can impact the volatility of markets at large, not to mention the individual stocks that are subject to those global macro events.

Individual stock option volatility levels (both historical and implied) can be found in sources like the CBOE. This is a great resource for seeing whether implied volatility for a security on which you are considering selling options is near a high or low vis-à-vis its historical range. For options sellers looking to optimize premiums earned, this is as useful as seeing whether a stock is trading near the high or the low of its P/E range.

Let's put things in perspective and wrap some science around the art. Historically, the **VIX**, which measures the near-term (30-day) expected volatility of the S&P 500 and thus is a tool for measuring **implied volatility**—as opposed to a **historical volatility**—has ranged between about 9 on the low end to just over 80 on the high end. An inverse correlation tends to exist between the VIX and the stock market: when the market drops fast, the VIX goes up; when the market goes up, the VIX drops. This holds true especially in the extremes. Whether the VIX is leading or following the market is unclear on any given day. However, when the VIX reaches extreme levels, it has proven to be an excellent contrarian indicator of future market movements. After being largely dormant for years, VIX spiked dramatically to over 80 (from under 20 in late 2019) in early 2020 as the pandemic started to unfold. The VIX can be thought of as a fear gauge; when people are afraid, when stocks are going down, when there is bad news on the front page of the *Wall Street Journal*, the VIX tends to be higher, and premiums for options (especially puts) are more expensive.

Volatility is neither absolute nor constant; it is ever-changing. A stock's historical volatility may be X whereas its implied volatility may be X + Y. An implied volatility that is higher than historical volatility might be driven by global macro factors, industry-level forces like new regulation, or company-specific forces like expected changes in management or the prospect of a takeover. For that matter, implied volatility might be, and often is, greater for puts than for calls, even on the same company. For example, if a stock is trading at $12.50 per share, you might think that call and put options on the stock with the same expiration date that are equally out-of-the-money ($10 puts that are 2.5 points OTM, and $15 calls that are also 2.5 points OTM) would have the same premium level. You should not be surprised, however, that premiums for puts are often more expensive than premiums for calls under this circumstance. People are willing to pay more to protect against the downside than they are to gain from the upside. Or, on a behavioral economic level that focuses on emotional drivers such as fear and greed, people hate to lose money more than they love to make money. Thus, put premiums are bid up higher than call premiums, especially during tumultuous times. This concept as depicted in Figure 4.11 is key to making profits so we will return to this later in depth.

### *Figure* 4.11 Asymmetrical Premium of Equidistant Calls and Puts

| Put Strike | Stock Price | Call Strike |
|---|---|---|
| $10.00 | $12.50 | $15.00 |
| ↓ | | ↓ |
| 20% OTM Put $2.30 Premium | | 20% OTM Call $1.40 Premium |

## THE PRICING OF OPTIONS

Now that we have learned the various macro issues that can impact volatilities in the stock market, let's discuss what micro considerations can affect the volatility of a given stock. For that we will go back to our insurance analogy.

Let's say you are considering buying fire insurance for your house. You live in a place with cold and wet winters and hot and dry summers. More fires start in the summer than in the winter because the brush and tinder that grows during the rainy season becomes dry and susceptible to flames during the summer. Since the probability of a fire is higher in the summer, a six-month policy covering April through September will be more expensive than one that extends from October to March. If a rash of fires breaks out in your area, premiums will rise. Want to have a policy to protect you for two years rather than six months? It will cost you more. Are you insuring a mansion or a small condominium? The house that is worth more will cost more to insure. These are the essential variables that go into the pricing of an option: the likelihood of the event occurring, the length of time being covered, and the value of the underlying asset.

But just how directly does movement in the value of an underlying security affect the prices of options? If a given stock moves 5%, will all its corresponding options also change 5% in value? Let's examine this question closely.

The term **delta** is defined as the amount an option price will change given a one-point change in the price of the underlying security. Delta values range from 0 to 1 for long call options and short put options (bullish options) and a value range of -1 to 0 for long puts and short calls (bearish bets). If a stock moves three points and the option delta is 1, the option will also move three points. While the exact calculation of delta is beyond the scope of this book (see www.thecompoundcode.com for information on where useful measurement tools can be found), as a rule of thumb, a stock that is **at-the-money (ATM)**—its price being at or near the option's strike price—will have a delta of approximately 0.5. As a stock's price moves farther and farther OTM—falling below strike price in the case of a call and rising above strike price in the case of a put—delta approaches 0. As a stock price becomes increasingly ITM—rising above the strike price in the case of a call and falling below the strike price in the case of a put—delta approaches 1.0 as shown in the following figure.

***Figure* 4.12 Short Put Deltas**

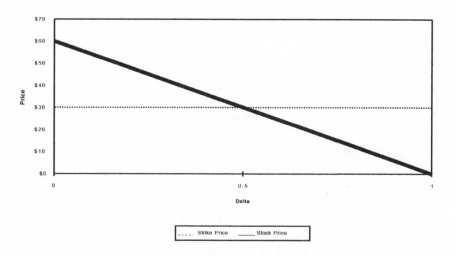

As shown in Figure 4.12, when the stock price is greater than $30, and the put is OTM, the delta approaches 0. When the stock price is less than $30, and the put is ITM, the delta approaches 1. When the option is ATM, with the strike price equaling the stock price, the delta is approximately 0.5. Compare this with the dynamics of deltas in the context of call options.

## *Figure* 4.13 Call Deltas

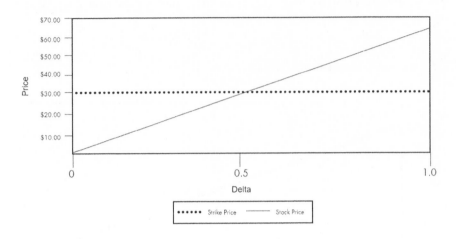

In the case of a call as noted in Figure 4.13, when the stock price is greater than $30, the call is ITM and the delta approaches 1. When the stock price is less than $30, and the call is OTM, the delta approaches 0. When the option is ATM, in this case when the stock equals the strike at $30, the delta is on the order of 0.5.

In effect, options self-regulate in that, as stock prices go down, your long exposure (via short puts) increases as deltas approach 1. Conversely, as a given stock price goes up and a short call becomes increasingly in-the-money, the short call delta approaches 1 and the combined position gets increasingly short. And that is the essence of buying low and selling high.

Here is an analogy to put the concept of deltas into perspective. Let's say you are playing tug-of-war. You start out with one person on each side, Person A on the left and Person B on the right. When Person A (the stock) tugs, Person B (the option or derivative) feels 100% of the effect of the tug. In this case, delta is 1, the option being fully ITM and behaving just as the underlying stock acts; the option 'feels' the full force of the stock's 'tug.' Now let's say we have twenty people on each side. When Group A pulls, the impact of this movement will still be felt almost entirely by the first few people in line in Group B. Will person twenty at the end of the line and perhaps fifty feet from the center—the position that is far out-of-the-money—be affected by the force of the tugs in the same way as the person near the center—at the strike price—will be? We know that those closest to the center will feel the tugs' effects more than those who are at the tail end of the tug-of-war game who have the equivalent of a delta far less than 1.

Another way to think about deltas is to consider the play in a steering wheel. If you are in an SUV and you turn the wheel, you will feel some looseness, or play, in the steering wheel. The steering wheel in your hand moves slightly before it causes the vehicle's wheels to turn. This would be the equivalent of a low delta, an option with a strike price that is far OTM relative to the underlying stock price. In contrast, if you are driving a high-end sports car then every movement in your shoulders and hands is transmitted to the steering wheel and then directly to the car's wheels. The yield of output to input is extremely high. This would be an in-the-money option with high delta values.

## NOTIONAL AND DELTA ADJUSTED EXPOSURES

In the world of stocks, **exposure** refers to the size of the 'bet.' Investing and trading in equities and options is nothing like gambling, but we'll use betting tables as an analogy only to bring clarity to a complex subject.

Let's say you go to Vegas with $100,000 in your pocket. If you step up to the roulette table and put all $100,000 on black, then you are 100% long black; you have 100% exposure to black. If you borrow $50,000 from the house and put $150,000 on black, then you have 150% exposure to black. If you put $50,000 on red and keep $50,000 in your pocket, you have 50% exposure to red. If you decide to sit out a spin of the wheel and make no bet at all, your exposure is 0%. This brings up two important concepts of exposure: gross and net. The former is the total of all long and short exposure, while the latter represents the addition of long and short exposure (short exposure being expressed as a negative value).

Using our roulette analogy, if you put $50,000 on black and $50,000 on red, your **total exposure** (aka **gross exposure**) would be 100%, but your net exposure would be 0% (not counting the green squares on the wheel). This is the equivalent of being neutral in the market, or having an equal amount of long exposure (hoping stocks will go up) and short exposure (wagering stocks will decline in price). Even with a neutral portfolio, you can still have lots of bets on the market. Of course, betting on both black and red on the same wheel makes no sense, as these two outcomes are mutually exclusive, the losses on one side of the transaction negating the gains on the other, whereas in the stock market your longs can go up concurrently with declines in shorts. But what if you were to line up dozens of roulette tables, each with an independent outcome? Now you could win on both your black bets and your red bets at the same time. Suppose that you had ten tables in front of you and that you knew half of them were tilted so that black came up more than 50% of the time, the other half of the tables being positioned so that red were the predominant outcome. In this case, you would put half your positions on black for the wheels that favored black and half your money on red on the wheels that favored red. You would have 100% exposure to the roulette wheel even though your net exposure was 0%. Your total roulette portfolio would be indifferent to whether black or red came up in general, as long as black came up on your black bets and red was the winner on your red bets. You could win simultaneously on black outcomes and red outcomes while not putting all your money on either black or red.

There are six ways to incur exposure in stocks and options. The three ways to attain long exposure are: (1) buying stocks long, (2) selling puts short, and (3) buying calls long. The three ways to get short exposure on your books are: (1) selling stocks short, (2) buying puts long, and (3) selling calls short. In equity investing, if you have a $100,000 portfolio and you buy $100,000 worth of the S&P 500 via an ETF like the SPYs, you have 100% long exposure. If you borrow $50,000 from your broker by going on **margin**, and you add it to your $100,000 of SPYs, then your total exposure is 150% long. If you buy $40,000 of the SPYs and keep the rest of your portfolio in cash, then you have 40% long exposure. If you take your entire $100,000 and short the SPYs, then your portfolio exposure is 100% short. Portfolio exposure can range from 100% or more short to 100% or more long (given the ability to borrow), and everything in between.

Hence, any given portfolio has gross (total) exposure, **gross long exposure**, **gross short exposure**, and **net exposure**. If you take the $100,000 portfolio described above that is 100% gross long via SPYs and sell short $40,000 of stocks that you think will underperform relative to the S&P 500, you have created a portfolio that has 140% gross total exposure (100% long exposure + 40% short exposure) but 60% net long exposure (100% long exposure minus 40% short exposure). In this scenario, though you have a long bias, you are relatively indifferent to the overall market direction *per se*; you just want your long bets to go up and your short bets to go down. One interpretation is that this portfolio is riskier than a 100% long-only portfolio in that your long exposure can go down and your short exposure can go up, with you losing both ways. A portfolio with 60% net long exposure will tend to decline less than the broad indices during down market conditions if the choice of underlying securities has been made intelligently.

If you wanted your portfolio returns to be independent of market direction and dependent solely on stock picks, you could go long $75,000 of certain stocks on which you were bullish, and short $75,000 of stocks you expected to decline, thereby setting up what is called a **market neutral** portfolio. In this case, though your portfolio gross exposure is 150%, your portfolio net exposure is 0%. Though you have placed more than 100% worth of bets, the total portfolio construction is theoretically more conservative than if you were 100% long the market (and certainly more conservative than if you were 150% long the market).

It is this ability to place more than 100% worth of bets while constructing a portfolio with a net exposure of less than 100% that allows sophisticated professional investors to outperform the market with less risk, a key concept explored in more detail below.

### Options Exposure

When you go long or short stocks, your exposure is long/short dollar for dollar the security being traded. The same does not hold true for options-induced exposure. Therefore, we need to introduce a few other types of exposure.

The first, **notional exposure**, can be defined as the total face value of the option if it were fully assigned. This is the equivalent of gross, or total, exposure for stocks. For instance, in the case of the purchase of ten Stock X $25 put contracts, the notional short exposure is $25,000. The purchase of five Stock X $30 calls would provide $15,000 of notional long Stock X exposure. The sale of twenty Stock X $22.50 puts would yield notional long exposure of $45,000, and so forth. Think of notional exposure as the face value of the contract.

But as we have learned, most options do not behave on a one-for-one basis with the underlying stock, so we must adjust the notional exposure for the delta of the option, giving us **delta adjusted exposure**—a very important concept for portfolio construction and risk management when options are involved. As noted, a stock with a price far out-of-the-money vis-à-vis the option strike price will have a delta close to 0. For example, if you have sold ten Stock X $25 puts when the stock is trading for $28 per share, the delta will be approximately 0.2. While the notional long exposure is $25,000, the delta adjusted exposure is only approximately $5,000. If the stock moves up $1, instead of your gaining $1,000 as you would if you owned 1,000 shares of Stock X long, your short put position will gain only $200, or 20% of the movement in the underlying security. Because the delta is 0.2, the option price will move only 0.2 points for every one point the stock moves. Similarly, if Stock X were to drop from $28 to $27, someone owning 1,000 shares of the stock long would lose $1,000 on his position, whereas the seller of ten short put contracts, while having the same notional exposure as the person owning the shares long, would lose only approximately $200. Note that for short call options and long put options, the delta is negative in that the option loses 20% of its value as the stock price rises. In other words, stock price and options price are inversely related in those two circumstances, whereas with short puts and long calls, a rise in the underlying stock also increases the value of the option.

*Figure* 4.14 **Portfolio Exposures**

---

**Sample Portfolio: $100,000**

1.  1,000 shares Co. X at $29 per share
    = 29% Gross Long

2.  1,000 shares Co. X at $29 per share + 5 contracts $30 short calls
    = 29% Gross Long + 15% Gross Short
    = 44% Total Gross

3.  1,000 shares Co. X at $29 per share + 5 contracts $30 short calls
    = 14% Net Long

---

There are other 'Greeks' like Vega, Gamma, and Theta which are beyond the scope of this book but which we review online at thecompoundcode.com.

## TIME VALUE

The notion that options are a wasting asset is an important one. Over time, the inherent value in options erodes (specifically the time value premium). The decline, however, is not linear but almost exponential.

For example, assume you buy an OTM put that has twenty days left until expiration. If time decay were linear, the option would lose 5% of its time value each day. Its intrinsic value will go up and down depending on how far ITM, if at all, the option is. But the option does not lose 5% of its value per day over those twenty days. Instead, it loses less than 5% per day in time value premium in the early days and more than 5% per day as the expiration date approaches.

Going back to the insurance analogy, let's say you were about to hop on a plane and an enterprising insurance salesman convinced you to buy flight insurance for $100 (the premium) for a four-hour flight (the expiration period). He then decided to join you on the flight and plopped down in the seat next to you. As a smart guy always looking to make a profit, he offers to buy the insurance back from you fifteen minutes into the flight, or 6% of the 240-minute flight time. If the decaying value of the insurance were linear, he would offer to buy the insurance back for approximately $94 since 6% of the flight minutes have elapsed. But being prudent and realizing a whole lot could still go wrong in the flight, you tell him you will only sell it back for $98. He declines, and you hold on to the insurance.

*Figure* **4.15 Time Decay of Options**

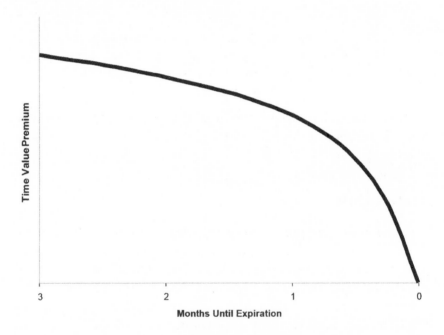

After a bad meal and a short film, the halfway point of the flight passes. Mr. Insurance turns to you and offers you $50 to buy back the insurance. "A fair deal," he says. "No way," you reply. "Even though the flight is halfway through, I still want to hedge against the event the insurance is protecting me from, so I'll only sell you the insurance back if you pay me $60." No deal.

The flight continues, the pilot informs you that you are well into your descent and that you should be on the ground and at the gate in about ten minutes. Buckle up those seat belts and turn off those mobile devices. "Ahh, we have made it," says Mr. Insurance. "I'll buy back your policy for two cents on the dollar—there are only ten minutes left in the flight, so you are lucky I'll pay you anything at all." "No way," you reply. "I'll take $15, or I am holding on. You know how tricky landings can be." "How about $8," he haggles. "That is double what my rate sheet says that I should pay you based on the fact that only 4% of the flight is left." Again, no deal.

Fortunately, your pilot is well trained, and the landing is smooth. Now you are confident that all will be okay, so you turn to Mr. Insurance to consummate a deal. After all, you have not been told "buh-bye" just yet, so you should be able to get something for your policy. But Mr. Insurance is on his cell phone, so you can't get his attention. "Can I sell you my policy for $10 now?" you ask as the plane comes to a peaceful stop and passengers start to gather their belongings. "How about $5?" you inquire desperately as you see the gateway approach the plane. Mr. Insurance is still on his phone . . . time is running out. The cabin door opens and passengers start filing out just as Mr. Insurance gets off the phone. "How about $2 to buy my policy back—I could still get hit in the noggin by some overhead baggage that shifted during flight." "I'll give you five cents," he replies. "But only ten minutes ago you were willing to pay me $8. How could the value have gone down so quickly?" "Tough break," beams Mr. Insurance as he quickly folds five crisp $20 bills into his pocket.

You have just learned the lesson of nonlinear time-value decay. In some cases, when earnings reports are released the evening before expiration, premiums hold much of their value until the bitter end—right up until expiration—driven largely by higher-than-average implied volatility right around earnings time. In that case, the time-decay graph appears even steeper than for most options expiration cycles as traders are willing to pay for options all the way up to expiration. Then, once the earnings news is released, options premiums collapse as traders conclude that extreme movements in the stock price are not in the cards. One conservative way to take advantage of this phenomenon is to sell at- or even in-the-money covered call options just prior to earnings. The profit stars align perfectly when earnings are announced close to options expiration which can actually yield a scenario where slightly ITM options provide strong annualized returns.

For example, if Company X is trading at $15.30 the day before it is to release earnings, you might be able to get $1 or more for the $15 calls about to expire in two weeks. Of course, fundamental analysis comes first, but if the company does not disappoint heavily, you have positioned yourself well—and conservatively—to earn a quick 5% raw return. Look out for these opportunities because they occur regularly if you are paying attention to the earnings calendar juxtaposed to the options expiration cycle.

## HOLIDAYS

Three-day weekends are beautiful things for sellers of options. Not just because they offer time to enjoy the beach on a summer holiday, but because the stock market's being closed represents a great source of profit for people who are short premium with time decay constantly working in their favor. Time is the friend of options sellers and the enemy of options buyers. You have probably heard the stock market adage "Sell in May and go away" that refers to professional investors' tendency to sell their book before heading to the Hamptons. And, not coincidentally, the traditional broad market summer doldrums are usually followed by a post–Labor Day year-end rally. In the case of options, any time you get a chance to put short premium on the books prior to a long weekend, sell on Friday and go away, all else being equal.

### *The Optimal Spot for Options Time Horizon*

What is the optimal time horizon for selling options? Thirty days? Sixty days? A year? First, some mathematical analysis. By definition, the return on an annualized, as opposed to absolute, basis is greater the nearer term the option is sold. Thus, while an investor will collect more absolute premium for calls sold ninety days out than for calls sold only thirty days out, the annualized return for the thirty-day calls is higher than that of the ninety-day calls given the accelerated decay toward the end of an option's life.

***Figure* 4.16 Option Time Frame Return Analysis**

| Days Until Expiration | Premium | Absolute Return | Annualized Return |
|:---:|:---:|:---:|:---:|
| 30 | $0.85 | 2.69% | 37.51% |
| 60 | $1.50 | 4.75% | 32.11% |
| 90 | $2.20 | 6.97% | 30.93% |

In addition to their greater annualized returns as noted in Figure 4.16, shorter-term options also provide more flexibility, in that they can be rolled, allowed to expire, or otherwise adjusted as needed with near-term broad market or stock-specific movements. Finally, the higher volume of nearer-term options traded means that their spreads tend to be narrower than the spreads of their long-dated counterparts with lower liquidity. That being said, practically speaking, longer dated options are often the way to go. Longer dated options offer similar return potential and allow you to ride out the short-term price volatility of the underlying security without either being called away or having the option expire far out of the money, both scenarios leaving you with no additional premium to earn on the given position.

What about **LEAPS**, or long-term equity anticipation securities? While OTM LEAPS puts are certainly a conservative way to enter a long-term stock position, they offer the combination of limited upside (limited to the amount of the premium sold) and all of the downside; the stock can go to zero. But if your bullish thesis were correct and the stock goes up over the long term, you do not participate in the gains beyond premium collected. By their nature, LEAPS offer little time-decay benefit in the near term, thus you get neither the advantage of near-term time decay nor the potential for capital appreciation inherent in longer-term equity holdings. LEAPS puts also offer less flexibility to take advantage of or respond to nearer-term broad market or company-specific events—actions that occur regularly and often present profit opportunities or reasons to become more defensive with regards to a given position. For example, if you sell near-dated OTM puts and the stock moves up on an expected earnings report, your less-than-sixty-day options might decline in value from $1 to $0.30 in a short period of time and allow you to buy them back at close to 80% of their profit potential. Then, if the stock declines again, you could resell puts for a higher premium level than your recent buy-to-close purchase. The same OTM LEAPS might drop in value from $3.50 to $3.20 and, given wide spreads typical for LEAPS, the repurchase of the put might be a break-even undertaking at best.

How far out timewise you sell an option might be driven by your return objectives; or it might be a function of the premium available at any given strike price. For example, let's assume you purchased Company X long at $22 per share and concurrently sold a thirty-day short call option with a strike price of $22.50 for $0.80 per contract. If the stock closes at $20 per share at time of expiration, you might need to go sixty, ninety or more days out to get a decent premium for the $22.50 strike price, the new thirty-day $22.50 call options having little to no premium left.

*Figure* **4.17 Near Versus Far OTM Return Profiles**

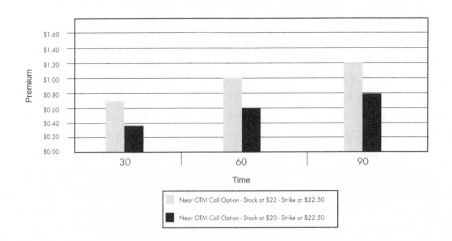

In this case, going out ninety days makes the most sense as this balances annual and absolute returns. When using options to add incremental profits to your core holdings, you can pick and choose your spots to collect premiums when the return profiles are favorable.

Key Takeaways:

- The mechanics of options can be convoluted at first. When used correctly, they can provide income generation as well as downside protection to a portfolio.
- Options can be exercised, closed out, left to expire, or rolled depending on the desired outcome in the portfolio.
- Though there are many ways to trade options in a portfolio, we recommend starting with covered calls (selling calls on equity positions held in the portfolio).
- The primary factors of options pricing are: time to maturity, underlying volatility, and the difference between the spot price and the strike price of the asset.

# CHAPTER 5

## OPTIMIZING OPTIONS

Now that we have learned the basics of options and the forces that drive their movements, let's look in more detail at practical ways to apply options to portfolio construction and trading.

### Selling Puts to Replace Assigned Stock

Let's say you purchased a stock for $48 per share and simultaneously sold the September $50 calls for $1.20 per share. At the time of expiration, the stock is trading at $50.30 per share, or slightly ITM. There is likely to be premium in the $52.50 later-dated strikes, so if you still feel bullish on the stock, you might want to close the September $50 calls for $0.40, or whatever they are trading for (still making $0.80 per share on the short calls) and roll into the October $52.50 contracts. This provides further upside capital gains potential while still offering some downside protection via the short call. And, if the ex-date for the company's next dividend is prior to the third Friday of October, then you have the potential to make money on the $52.50 calls, the stock, and the dividend. This is a nice triple treat. The farther OTM the call option sale is, the 'looser' the hedge is and the more you are relying on capital appreciation for gains. By contrast, at or near-the-money calls provide a 'tighter' hedge that shifts profit potential away from capital gains and towards premium collection.

**POWER TIP**

**Avoiding Pre-Mature Assignments**

Often you will own a dividend-paying stock long and be short covered calls against the security that become ITM. The person on the other side of your short call position—the owner of the call—will likely want to exercise his option to purchase the stock (now that the stock price is above the strike price) at a time when he can capture the dividend. Therefore, if your goal is to hold on to the stock and earn the upcoming dividend, be sure to either close your short call option position entirely or roll it to a higher strike price or a later-dated option or both—or risk getting burned by the looming ex-date. The only saving grace in getting prematurely assigned on an option, be it due to the buyer of the option looking to capture the dividend or the option simply being so deep in the money prior to expiration that the buyer of the option chooses to exercise, is that at least you are earning the entire profit potential on the position in less than the expected option period. Thus, your annualized returns increase because your holding period has been shortened.

What if the stock price is $52 approaching expiration? You do not want to roll to the $52.50 calls, but you would have to go too far out timewise to get a decent delta premium on the $50 strike price. In other words, since the option is well in-the-money, there will be very little time value premium in the later-dated $50 calls. One technique is to sell puts to replace the stock that was just (or is about to be) **called away**. If you purchased 1,000 shares at $48 per share and sold the September $50 calls for $1.20, your effective sale price is $51.20 at time of **assignment** and your total profit is $3.20 per share, or 7% ROI **raw**. Rather than rolling the calls for little to no time premium, you can sell the October $50 puts, likely collecting another $1 to $2 per share of premium. Thus, if the stock price drops and you are subsequently assigned, you would buy the stock at the equivalent of $50 minus the premium you collected, or $48.50 per share if you got $1.50

for the puts. This is a more conservative, effective, and potentially profitable way of maintaining exposure to a covered call position that has become ITM at expiration. At times stocks trade in ranges. Within a portfolio of twenty to thirty stocks, certain positions are stronger and others weaker at any given time, either for transitory but fundamental reasons (such as an industry performing better during certain parts of the economic cycle), or for nonfundamental reasons that are reflected in the market regularly. Taking advantage of the ranges—effectively and repeatedly buying more shares when the price is lower and selling them when the price is higher, either directly or by way of short options—can add incremental profits to a portfolio while lowering risk.

## POWER TIP
### The Covered Call Return Profiles

What types of annualized returns should one look for between dividends, capital appreciation, and options premiums when considering selling covered calls? While everyone has a different perspective and risk/reward profile, a good starting point is if the sale of a call leads to a position with 15% or more annualized upside, then the call is worth selling. The 15% annualized return can be made up of any combination of capital gains (or even a loss, if the call option sold is in-the-money), dividends, and the option premium itself. Remember that the sale of a call provides the additional benefit of some downside protection, so even if a 15% annualized return figure seems too small in and of itself, you need to give the position credit for the fact that it has less risk than an unhedged long-only stock holding. Therefore, if you purchase a stock for $24.50 per share and sell a $25 strike price call for $0.85 which expires in three months' time, the annualized return potential for this position is approximately 26% assuming the stock has a 4% yield. When VIX is very high, the annualized returns a trader can get from fairly tight call sales can exceed a 15% annualized return objective, so take advantage of these rich premiums on high-quality companies.

## Delta Premium

In general, maximum delta premium credit occurs when the stock is at or very near the strike price sold. When there is still time before expiration, there is always a trade-off between capturing additional time decay in the option you currently hold short, and the loss in delta time premium the more a given stock becomes ITM. The closer to expiration, the more the position has captured all possible time decay, thus the more important it is to roll when the option becomes ATM or ITM. The optimal outcome is that a stock closes just below a given strike price (in the case of a short call) or just above (in the case of a short put). This scenario allows you to capture the entire directional and time premium for your current short option, and in turn to sell the next dated option at its maximum premium for your chosen strike price.

If you have let a short put get ITM and are considering rolling it to a later-dated expiration date to avoid getting prematurely assigned as well as to capture at least some delta premium credit, you are in essence making a bet on what the stock price will do between today and expiration. Let's say you are short April $90 puts on Company X, which is now trading at $85 a few days before expiration. Your puts are trading for about $6.20 per share, the intrinsic value of $5 + $1.20 of the remaining time premium. A few days before expiration you could close the puts for $6.20 and sell the next month's same strike price options for about $8.50, or a delta credit of $2.30.

Three basic things could happen between now and expiration if you decide not to roll the option today but rather to wait until closer to expiration (with the intention of rolling the option if it is still ITM). First, the underlying stock price could head farther south, and you could wake up one morning to find yourself prematurely assigned. In this case, you either hold the stock long and unhedged, immediately sell calls against the position (there will likely be good premiums in the $90 calls not-too-far dated), or sell the stock and reenter a later-dated short put option to replace the stock. This is the worst-case scenario because you will likely have little, if any, delta premium credit.

The second possible scenario is that the stock moves very little and you roll for a delta premium before being assigned (whether at expiration date or before). This is the middle best case. The optimal scenario is that the underlying stock rallies as expiration nears. The closer the stock price approaches the strike price, in this case $90 per share, the higher your delta credit will be as noted in Figure 5.1. The scenario in which you make maximum profits is the one in which the stock closes at $90.01 so that your cost to close the position is $0 (it expires worthless) and you get the maximum premium for selling the next-dated options.

**Figure 5.1 Delta Credit Premiums at Various ITM Scenarios**

| Stock Closing Price | Delta Credit Premium | April Premium (Closing Cost) | May Premium | Return on Investment |
|---|---|---|---|---|
| $90.00 | $3.75 | $0.00 | $3.75 | 4.17% |
| $89.50 | $3.40 | $0.60 | $4.00 | 3.80% |
| $89.00 | $3.10 | $1.10 | $4.20 | 3.48% |
| $88.50 | $3.00 | $1.60 | $4.60 | 3.39% |
| $85.00 | $0.50 | $5.10 | $5.60 | 0.59% |

## Doubling Up, Doubling Down

If you have sold a naked put or covered call that clearly is well OTM approaching expiration, you can 'double up' your position for the short period of time prior to expiration by writing the option again for a future expiration date. In this way, you are effectively getting decay for both options by not buying back the option that is presumably about to expire worthless. For example, if you earlier sold September $45 strike price puts on a stock that is trading at $47 per share the day before expiration, you may opt to sell October (or whatever the next options expiration date is) $45 strike price puts even before the September options expire. When you are the seller of premium, the longer the premium is on the books, the more time is working on your side. By selling the next month's options on the Thursday before expiration, rather than waiting until Monday post-expiration, you get an additional three to four days of time decay working for you. All things being equal, the next month's option will probably lose ten to fifteen cents' worth of premium between Thursday and Monday (which could easily be 10% or more of the position). If your goal is to squeeze intelligently every penny of profit then doubling up is a good idea. The same applies to doubling up on short calls that are well OTM going into expiration.

**POWER TIP**
**When to Hold 'Em, When to Fold 'Em**

Sometimes your options hand is strong, sometimes it is weak. It is important to take the right actions to optimize your profit potential. Here are two scenarios. If you hold an ITM short put that is approaching expiration and the option becomes less ITM for some reason, you are well served to use this strength to roll the option to a later-dated strike price. While you might get lucky and the underlying stock continues to rise so that the option ends up worthless at expiration, it is best to take advantage of this strength to roll and get the large delta premium credit while you can (prior to expiration). If the stock does continue to rally, you will be making money on your later-dated short puts. If, however, the stock heads back south prior to expiration, you will have lost the opportunity to get any meaningful delta premium credit. Thus, rolling on strength provides only upside while hesitating can lead to a situation in which little to no premium credit is attained as the options become increasingly ITM. Discipline, as always, is key. Conversely, if the short put is slightly OTM approaching expiration, it is okay to hold the position until expiration approaches as the option will at best expire worthless (stay OTM) or at worst get closer to ATM or even slightly ITM—in which case substantial delta premium credit will still be available.

As with all investing and trading, however, it is important to know what your true risks are and to manage them accordingly. Stock prices can move quickly and dramatically, often when you least expect it. It is not uncommon for even large-cap stocks to move 5% or more in a single day. It is one thing to dash to your bathroom without any clothes on in the privacy of your home; it is another thing entirely to run down the street naked.

When selling additional further-dated puts on top of the puts you are already short—the ones about to expire—you are adding incremental long exposure to your portfolio. You need to be prepared to act very quickly if the stock goes against you, or to take on the additional exposure if the stock price that was well out-of-the-money on Thursday suddenly falls below the strike price on the Friday of expiration. Again, this does not happen often, but it does happen. Knowing what is on the calendar—earnings announcements, Fed meetings, and the like—is vital, as these events might drive near-term stock movements. Having an alert system in place is also critical so that if the stock hits a certain predetermined target, you can close out the option that is about to expire before it starts losing you money. One good technique is to establish an e-mail alert that notifies you when a stock on which you have doubled up on $22.50 puts hits $23.50.

Depending on how close to expiration it is (and how averse you are to being assigned on the puts such that the size of your effective position doubles), a trigger of 2% to 5% away from the strike price is a good range. That way, you can close your about-to-expire $22.50 puts while they're still profitable.

If you are unable to monitor the position, then do not double up on options prior to expiration; it is simply not worth the risk that the one time you are unable to act quickly a dramatic market or stock movement will take place. A single material event can result in a loss that wipes out your other gains and then some. Imagine if you were holding a covered call position on a meme stock in 2021 and decided to pre-sell the following month's options since the stock was well below the about to expire option. The next day the stock jumps 30% and your formerly profitable position turns decidedly unprofitable as you become essentially short the stock with the extra naked short call position. It is never worth trying to pick up nickels on the highway if there has been a history of big trucks coming out of nowhere at 100 MPH.

After selling incremental options on about-to-expire positions, you will soon get a feel for the relationship between the number of days left until expiration, how far OTM the option is, and what trigger price should cause you to close out the about-to-expire option while still preserving your position profit. Clearly, the closer to expiration, the closer the stock price can be to the strike price and allow you to double up. If expiration is due in a few minutes and the stock price in question is 2% or more from the strike price, you can pretty safely sell the incremental calls/puts, although you should be prepared to monitor the position until close to be certain, because even a quick flash can get you in trouble. Similarly, the farther away the stock price is from the strike price, the more room for error you have in doubling up (always with an alert in place). As with all trading, this is part art (pattern recognition, a gut feel for stock movements, and a sense of time decay) and part science (doing the math), and only with experience will you develop the necessary skills.

*Figure* **5.2 Managing Option Positions**

|  | Option Near Expiration | Option Far from Expiration |
|---|---|---|
| Stock Far from Strike | OPTIMAL<br>Doubling Up OK | Moderate Risk<br>Monitor Doubling via Alerts |
| Stock Near Strike | Moderate Risk<br>Monitor Doubling via Alerts | DANGEROUS<br>Focus on Risk Control |

In supervising options positions around expiration, other risk considerations include total portfolio exposure, net exposure, and position size. Let's say you have purchased 500 shares of Company X for $23 per share and sold five of the September $25 strike price calls. Soon after you purchase the stock it falls to $21 per share, so you take this opportunity to **layer in** more long exposure by selling five of the $20 September puts, bringing your total notional long exposure to the equivalent of 1,000 shares long excluding the OTM short calls, which reduces your net position exposure slightly. For this example, assume that your portfolio size is $1 million so that your notional long position size is 2.05% (500 shares at $21 per share, the current price, plus 500 shares at $20 per share via the short puts). Of course, your delta adjusted long exposure is less than 2.05% since the delta on the puts about to expire is close to zero and your short calls reduce your long exposure, but for the purpose of this analysis, it is best to use the more conservative notional exposure calculations (for many accounts, short puts are secured by cash meaning that the brokerage firm sets aside the notional value of the option and reduces margin availability commensurately).

If, shortly before expiration, the stock is trading around $22 and you are confident that the short September put position will expire worthless, you might elect to sell five October $20 puts before September expiration to take advantage of additional time decay. In this case, your notional long exposure will increase from 2.05% to 3.05% (500 shares at $21 per share plus ten short puts at $20 per share). An important variable to consider for risk control is the total position size on a notional basis. Remember, when selling options, you have to think the same way as the buyer or seller of a stock: how are the fundamentals of the business? What is the valuation? In terms of portfolio construction, how big is the position? When calculating the latter figure—and, indeed, for ongoing portfolio construction and managing purposes—using delta adjusted figures is perfectly legiti- mate. When making incremental exposure decisions, however, you are best served by focusing on the more conservative notional exposures. Remember, the purpose of risk control is to consider what will happen in the worst-case scenarios should the proposed position work against you. It is not a matter of if, but when, you will experience a dramati- cally adverse move, so you need to plan accordingly and not end up with unintentionally large single-company positions.

It is one thing if the total notional short put exposure for the posi- tion is 4% via doubling your puts prior to expiration; it is another matter entirely if the sale of the additional puts increases the notional position size from 5% to 10%. In this case, you are likely better served by waiting to write additional puts until you are nearly, if not totally, certain that the September puts will expire worthless—waiting until just before close Friday or even until the following Monday post- expiration. *When in doubt, choose the conservative approach, which is to hold off on selling the incremental puts.* Remember, your goal is to optimize overall portfolio performance, not to maximize every trade.

Attempting to maximize every single position might lead to a subopti-
mal total outcome over time.

At times your short puts will continue to go against you so that you
have to keep rolling them as they get deeper and deeper ITM. Once a
short put gets deep ITM, approximately 9% or more, delta approaches
1.0 and you are effectively long the stock as noted in Figure 5.3.

*Figure* **5.3 ITM Short Put Deltas**

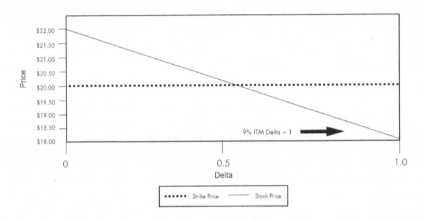

At that point you might want to sell short calls at the same strike
price to hedge the position and add incremental profits to your portfolio. Remember, however, that your short puts provide no profit
potential above the strike price, so your short calls will become naked
if the price of the stock goes above the strike price. Furthermore, you
will likely have to go out sixty days, ninety, or more days out since you
will be selling calls at the same strike price as your ITM puts.

In this case, you must place premium on the books as soon as possible to get time decay working for you. Of course, the downside to
selling the short calls so far out in time is that the underlying stock
might rebound in the interim. Consider selling short calls selectively
against deep ITM short put positions and setting alerts so that if the
stock gets to within approximately 5% of the strike price (depending
on how far from expiration), you can close the short call so that the net
exposure on the position will not become negative if the underlying

stock price continues to rise. This is noted in Figure 5.4. Alternatively, you can put on a partial hedge, specifically selling fewer short calls than puts that you are short. A 2:1 ratio of puts to calls is a conservative way to go and will ensure that the combined position stays net long except and until the underlying stock increases dramatically, at which point your alert would have long since notified you to take action accordingly.

*Figure* **5.4 Alert Setting: Short Calls Against ITM Short Puts**

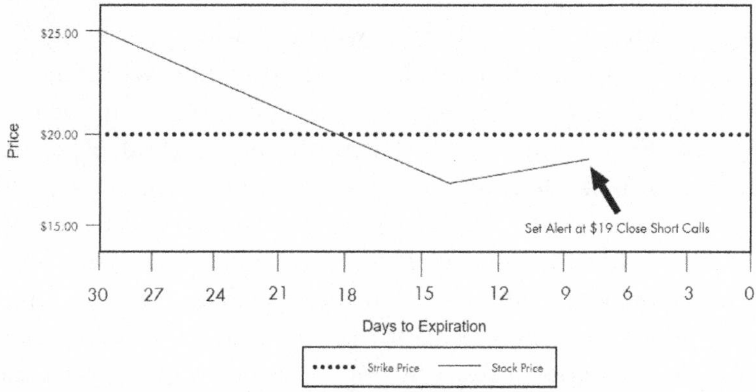

When you are short both puts and calls on a given security (without any direct ownership), another way to look at your effective net position exposure is to examine absolute premium dollar levels rather than, or in addition to, delta adjusted exposure levels. These premium levels can be a good proxy for delta adjusted exposure levels. Thus, if you have $3,200 of short put exposure and $800 of short call exposure, you still have a net long position (even if you have more short calls on the books than short puts on a notional contract basis).

## Ratio Call Selling

There are times when you own a stock long against which you sold a call that subsequently dropped materially in value due to the substantial decline of the long stock position. If VIX is high or the volatility of the underlying stock is significant, opportunities to sell calls on a 2:1 or even 3:1 notional basis will arise. This is sometimes called **ratio call selling**. As depicted in Figure 5.5, let's say you purchased 1,000 shares of Company X on March 3 for $28 per share and immediately sold ten contracts of the June $30 calls that are about three months out for $1.55 per contract. About halfway through the options cycle the stock is trading at $24.50 per share and your call options have collapsed in price to $0.40 due to time decay and directional decline. You still believe this is a quality company, and it pays a dividend that you are collecting. One strategy is to write additional calls seventy-five to ninety days farther out, in this case ten contracts (or fewer, to be more conservative) of the July $30 calls for $1.10. Since deltas will be very low on the way OTM calls, the net position will still be long—up to a point. With time decay on your side, anything short of a massive, sudden run-up in the underlying stock will put you ahead by having double short call exposure on the books. As stocks do run up quickly from time to time, always use a good alert system so that you can close the incremental calls at a profit if need be. In this case, an initial alert price at approximately $27 per share will allow you to still close out the June $30 options at a profit. (In general, you want to close out the premium at 50% of the original sale price at most, in this case approximately $0.80 per contract). Certainly, as June expiration approaches and the June options begin to decay dramatically, you can slowly increase your alert price to $28 and then ultimately to $29. The trade-off for selling the incremental calls is that you gain more by getting a later-dated premium on the books than you might lose by having to close out your nearer-dated options at a higher price. Short of a takeover (which does happen periodically, so be prudent), this is a fairly conservative way to gain incremental market exposure and profits, as long as you are disciplined with your alerts and buybacks.

A scenario you will face often occurs when you have purchased stock long and sold call options which you believe are about to expire worthless. You decide to do sell the next-dated October options to get additional exposure on the books. Let's say your covered calls are Septembers which expire in a few days and the stock starts heading north rapidly. Which options should you close? Since the October calls you just sold still have substantial time premium in them whereas the September calls have virtually none, you are better off closing the September rather than the October calls.

In essence, the trade-off of doubling up on calls is that the incremental premium gained by selling the later-dated option prior to expiration rather than after expiration outweighs any potential gain in the stock that would (1) cause you to have to close your about-to-expire option or (2) would have allowed you to sell the option for more premium at a later date (due to the rising stock price having increased the later-dated premiums).

## *Figure* 5.5 Ratio Call Selling

| March 3, 2023 | April 21, 2023 |
|---|---|
| 1  Buy 1,000 shares Co. X at $28/share<br>2  Sell 10 June $30 Calls for $1.55<br><br>**Portfolio**<br>Stock: $28,000<br>Short (June) Calls:($12,600)<br><br>Net Exposure: $15,400 | 1  Sell 10 July $30 Calls for $1.1<br>2  Set Price Alert at $27 for June Calls<br><br>**Portfolio**<br>Stock: $24,500<br>Short (June) Calls: ($5,100)<br>Short (July) Calls: ($8,400)<br><br>Net Exposure: $11,000 |
| **May 19, 2023** | **June 16, 2023** |
| 1  Set Price Alert at $28 for June Calls<br><br>**Portfolio**<br>Stock: $25,000<br>Short (June) Calls: ($2,400)<br>Short (July) Calls: ($5,400)<br><br>Net Exposure: $17,200 | 1  Set Price Alert at $29 for June Calls<br><br>**Portfolio**<br>Stock: $27,500<br>Short (June) Calls: ($1,200)<br>Short (July) Calls: ($5,700)<br><br>Net Exposure: $20,600 |

If indeed the stock does 'pop,' don't make the mistake of hoping the stock will come back down and allow you to hold both the September (to full expiration) and October calls. You might get lucky with the stock closing below the strike price at expiration, but this possibility is not worth the risk. If you do not close out your September calls immediately, your stock may be called away upon expiration, leaving you with October naked calls. At this point, you are effectively short the stock. Since your portfolio should be full of only top-quality companies, that would mean that you are short a great company that is trading at a reasonable valuation and that's not a good position to take. Assuming the sale of puts is done on quality companies at good valuations and your total notional exposure is such that the position size is reasonable, doubling up on short puts can be an effective way to squeeze out incremental profits prior to expiration because the downside associated with doing so is limited with time on your side. But the sale of incremental short calls prior to expiration should be done carefully and selectively—and if the position begins to work against you, it should be unwound immediately. Focus on the forest, not a leaf on a tree. It is not a contest of you against a single stock price at a moment in time: keep the big picture in mind and the purpose of your options strategies.

## THE IMPACT OF EVENTS ON PREMIUMS

Individual stock volatility can heighten dramatically in the days before earnings releases, only to collapse once the figures have been made public. Because earnings are an important variable in determining whether a stock will move through a given strike price, the anticipation of this data point and its release can have a big impact on options premium levels. Accordingly, the main variable to consider when contemplating options moves around expiration is whether the temporarily high premium levels driven by earnings uncertainty will outweigh any directional gains or losses after earnings release.

Assume you own a stock long that is trading at $33.20 on a Tuesday in April before the company is to release its earnings on Thursday before the open. Friday is options expiration day. You are short the $35 April calls, which are now trading for only a few pennies. One move is to take advantage of the enhanced premiums associated with the pending earnings announcement and sell the May $35 or even $37.50 (to allow for more upside) calls now (either closing your April contracts concurrent with the sale of the May options or doubling up on the calls with a very tight alert around $34 in case earnings come in above expectations and the stock rallies hard on Thursday). The sale of May options with the concurrent closing of the April contracts would be the conservative trade. If earnings are disappointing the stock will either be flat or down and you will have maximized the premium you received for selling the May $35/$37.5 calls as they will likely trade down based on the combination of: (1) time decay (the fact that a couple of days have passed), (2) directional decay (the fact that the stock has declined in price), and (3) reduced volatility (the fact the volatility-induced premium has dropped with the announcement of earnings).

**POWER TIP**

**The Battle of the Ages**

The way to think about the counterbalancing forces of time decay and the strengthening of the underlying stock price is as follows: As we age, we lose a certain amount of physical strength and endurance. After the age of approximately thirty-five, if you do not exercise at all, you lose a given percentage of your muscle and aerobic capacity each year. If you exercise, this exertion helps to offset the natural deterioration of the body. To make the analogy clear, think of physical exercise as an increasing stock price and time as . . . well, time. In the case of a stock rising rapidly just prior to expiration, the company is working out very hard. However, time is against its about-to-expire options, the ones 'near the end.' For the farther time-dated options, the ones with a longer life ahead of them, the increase in stock price, just like a good workout program, can have a positive impact on the options' price and health. For options nearing the end of their life, however, time tends to win the battle. You can work out as much as you want, but if you are on your deathbed, exercise has little effect.

Under the scenario in which you have sold May calls prior to earnings being announced (and maintained your April calls) and the

company announces favorable earnings—both historical and projected—you need to act quickly to close out your April calls. While
this would not be the optimal outcome relative to your timing of May
call sales, assuming you close out your April calls before the stock rises
too much, it is still a favorable outcome for your portfolio.

The more aggressive trade would be to wait until earnings are
announced and adjust your options concurrently with the subsequent
stock reaction. If earnings are strong and the stock rallies, you will generally be able to buy your April calls back for pennies (since time decay
is so dramatic in the last day or two approaching expiration), and get
maximum premium for May options to boot, given the increase in
price of the underlying stock. See Figure 5.6 for a depiction of this
effect. Options give you the flexibility and precision to have predetermined outcomes based on your thesis about upcoming events.

**Figure 5.6 Varying Effects of a Rising Stock Price on Options**

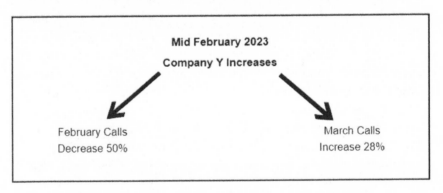

In mid-February 2023, Company Y increased 7.27% from $20.91
to $22.43 on positive earnings news. This caused the March calls to
increase by about 28%, whereas February options due to expire in a
few days actually declined around 50%. This scenario provides a stark
example of near-term options decay.

**POWER TIP**

**Optimization Defined**

We frequently used the term 'optimize' rather than 'maximize.' This usage is not accidental. As investors and traders, we make decisions regularly. Absent risk/reward considerations, we would likely always think in terms of maximizing our results. If you are naked some way OTM calls going into expiration, the maximized result is to let them expire worthless—and thus not have to pay the nickel and commission to buy the options back. However, this maximizing choice might not be the optimal approach. Remember, our portfolio is the aggregate of our investment and trading decisions over long periods. Therefore, many times non-maximizing choices lead to overall optimal outcomes. Keep this in mind when you are trying to squeeze every penny out of a trade—or when you hold a given position only because you feel you need to 'beat the market and not lose the battle against this stock. Focus on the war, not the individual battles, and you will come out ahead in the end.

## CALCULATING ROI ON OPTION SALES

How can you best calculate the return on investment on options positions? For covered calls, the answer is simple. The ROI is the sum of the capital gains, premium received, and any dividend collected (minus margin interest paid if the stock was purchased using leverage) divided by the stock purchase price. For example, if you purchased Company X for $43 per share and simultaneously sold the $45 strike price calls for $1.10, your return upon assignment would be $3.10 ($2 capital gain plus $1.10 premium collected) divided by $43, or 7.2%. If you collected a $0.50 dividend as well, your gross (also known as absolute or raw) return would increase to 8.4%.

You can look at this return on an absolute basis (the actual return on a percentage basis) or an annualized basis. Assuming you held the position for three months (the calls you sold simultaneously with the long equity purchase were ninety days out), then the annualized return would be approximately 34%, depending on whether you look at this on a compounded or additive basis. Be careful, however, about annualized return claims as they assume the particular position is replicable every time period held. Traders who are new to options often comment that they were told by firms selling options-related trading software that they can make X% (usually 4% to 6%) monthly via a covered call options strategy. While it might be true that for any particular position for a given thirty-day time period the potential return is 5%, repeating this return profile on the same security every thirty days is virtually impossible. By their nature, stocks rarely close right below the strike price at which you sold the option (which would yield the highest possible return for the time period), making it possible for you to rewrite the option for additional maximum premium. If such a stock did close month after month at or near a given strike price, it would have a very low volatility profile and the premium you would receive for selling options against such a stock—and, in turn, the return potential for said position—would drop over time. To be sure, high-volatility stocks are typically cited in claims of 5% monthly return potential, and volatility cuts both ways. Only one significant drop in a company's stock price is needed to quickly eliminate the following month's 5% options related return potential. For short put options, the calculations are a bit more complex if not inexact. Simply stated, there is no universally accepted approach to calculating ROI on the sale of put options. For easy math, assume the portfolio in question is valued at $1,000,000. Ten OTM puts are sold on Company X at $100 strike price for $1 per contract, providing $1,000 of premium. What is the ROI for this position if the option expires worthless and the maximum profit of $1,000 is reached? Let's examine four possible calculations, all done on a raw (not annualized) basis and determine which methodology best represents true returns:

1. ROI = $1,000/$1,000,000, or 0.10%. This calculation expresses the position profit over the total portfolio/capital base. I think this is *not* the best way to look at the profit of the position as the ROI should relate to the position-specific capital outlay and not to the total portfolio. Ultimately, we want to see how profitable

the position is—not how much profit it adds to the portfolio (though portfolio profitability relates to total capital amounts at the beginning and end of any given time period).

2. ROI = $1,000/$100,000, or 1%. This approach examines the premium received relative to the notional value of the short puts (ten contracts X 100 shares per contract at $100 per share, or $100,000). The notional value of the short put position is the amount of capital outlay needed if the option were assigned, or full attribution of capital. Hence, in this case the ROI would be 1% raw.

3. ROI = $1,000/margin capital used up. For most brokerage accounts, depending on how far OTM the put is, and on other variables, the sale of a naked put will use up about 25% of buying power available on a notional basis, so in this case you are using up about $25,000 of 'gunpowder' (25% of $100,000). Thus, the return here is $1,000/$25,000, or 4% raw.

4. ROI = incremental profit or infinite profit. This is an interesting way of looking at the profits. The rationale here is that you have your core portfolio, perhaps even 100%, invested. On top of that you layer in incremental OTM put positions that add to the P&L *ad infinitum*. Clearly there is a limit, however, to the number of puts one can sell based on capital levels and margin requirements, so this line of reasoning should not be taken to the extreme. The profit is neither 'free' nor unlimited from a cash-available or risk standpoint, so one can't truly say that the ROI is infinite. There must be a base by which to divide the profit. In a declining market, this theoretical infinite profit can become a very real loss; the idea that the sale of OTM short puts is 'free money' and adds infinite incremental ROI to a portfolio is a tenuous one at best.

While there is no right or wrong answer *per se*, the most accurate calculation of ROI is probably #3, or some blend of #2 and #3. At the end of the day, what matters is the return of a total portfolio within the context of risk taken. That should be your focus, though you should certainly consider the ROI for any given option position for risk management purposes and position sizing.

## Selling Options on ETFs vs. Individual Stocks

Some people like to use an options-writing strategy with a single broad-based ETF like the SPYs. The thinking is that you are getting enough diversification with the S&P 500, which is easier to track, and that you don't need to worry about individual stock selection. While these are valid points, and for long-term buy-and-hold investors a portfolio with a small number of low-cost, broad-based ETFs or mutual funds can be a great approach, for the more active trader looking to add incremental profit to a portfolio, there is a potentially superior strategy.

Let's use DIAs in our example. As a starting point, you buy the DIA ETF and sell calls against it at whatever level OTM meets your objectives (tight calls for more income and downside protection, farther OTM calls for more capital gains potential). Thirty days later the ETF closes just below your given strike price and you repeat the cycle. That all sounds good...except that in most cases the DIAs will close well below the option strike price or perhaps even well in-the-money. What do you do then? If you bought the DIAs for $342.50 and sold the next month's $345 calls for $3.20 and DIA closes at $321.35 so that the following month's $345 calls have virtually no premium in them, then what are your alternatives? You can sell an option that expires in thirty days at a strike price low enough to give you decent premium, for example the $325 calls. This, however, locks you into a loss should the DIAs rebound and force an assignment. Alternatively, you can sell the $345 calls but at an expiration date that is six months or farther away. In either case, you are tied to the semi-random closing price of a single security. You might have to wait several months, not selling and collecting options premium in the interim, until the ETF price 'comes to you' thus allowing you to begin to sell options premium again at strike prices that fulfill your gain objectives.

Compare the purchase of a basket of stocks (even the thirty securities contained in the Dow Jones 30 Industrials). In a twenty-to-thirty position portfolio, some positions invariably close near the strike prices (which is optimal in terms of maximizing future premium sold). Some close ITM so that you are called away and thus the profit potential drops from, say, three percent monthly to zero since this position is no longer in the portfolio. And other stocks close well OTM, the next month's premium for the same strike price being low or nonexistent. Given that you have a basket of stocks, however, you can sell the same strike price puts on your buy-write positions that have closed ITM for the next month to maintain exposure to the security. For the stocks that closed slightly OTM, you can sell the same strike price for a later-dated option and maximize premium earned. For those long equity positions for which your call expired well out-of-the-money, you could capture capital gains by owning the stock unhedged or wait until the stock price increases to sell additional calls. You could even lower your average purchase price by acquiring additional shares at lower prices (or by selling OTM puts) assuming you are comfortable with the combined position size. For incremental share purchases, consider selling ATM or even ITM calls since the first tranche of shares purchased are now unhedged.

Simply put, the Monday after options expiration offers all sorts of opportunities to profit when you are working with a basket of stocks that have closed at various levels relative to option strike prices that expired two days before. To be sure, part of you will want Monday to open up on weakness so that the stock that was assigned away over the weekend can be bought back at lower prices. Other parts of you will hope for strength so that call premiums will be richer on stocks for which OTM calls have just expired. In any case, you will invariably have a variety of opportunities to optimize profits within this dynamic portfolio, one of the many advantages of maintaining a portfolio with twenty to thirty positions rather than just selling options against a single or few broad-based ETFs. Be certain to have alerts set up to inform yourself in real time if a particular stock price has gone down to a certain price or if a certain security has reached a sale price. That way you will know that stocks have either opened sharply higher or lower - and can be ready to take advantage once again of whatever near-term prices the market has to offer post expiration.

**POWER TIP**

**Only the Shadow**

A shadow short is one way to look at an OTM put. If you sell a put with a strike price of $20 when the underlying stock is trading at $23 per share, you have a "shadow short" between $23 and $20. Unlike a real short, you do not profit from a decline in the stock, but you do not lose money if the stock rises. On the contrary, you make money as the stock price increases. By selling the OTM put, you are saying that you are not a buyer of the stock until it gets to your strike price; hence you are holding a shadow short.

## ADDITIONAL OPTIONS TRADING TIPS

Below are some frequently asked questions about situations that arise when trading options.

*If I am bullish on a given stock but I am looking to just make a trade as opposed to investing in the company for the long term, am I better off buying the stock long and selling a call or selling a put with the equivalent notional exposure?*

The risk/reward ratio of entering a covered call position versus a naked put position depends on several variables. First, in general, puts offer more premium than calls that are equally OTM. Therefore, if a stock is trading evenly between two strike prices, then the sale of a put will generally offer a better return potential on a risk/reward basis whereas the buy write has greater total gains potential.

### Selling Put Versus Buying Stock/Selling Call

Specifically, assuming Company X stock is trading right between two strike prices at $21.25 a share, selling the $20 puts might provide $1 per share of return potential and lower your effective purchase price to $19 per share (reduce risk). The purchase of shares long combined with the sale of a $22.50 call for $0.90 per share will provide for a return potential of $2.15 per share but your breakeven will be $20.35, or nearly 7% higher than under the put sale scenario. Thus, if you have more conviction on the stock, enter a buy write whereas if you are looking to be more conservative, sell the puts. Given the deltas associated with the OTM puts, you can actually sell more puts to generate similar profits as the buy write setup. You would have to approximately double your notional exposure (sell twice as many contracts) to generate the same absolute profit as buying the stock long and selling an equally OTM call. Thus, you are ultimately looking at risk reward ratios.

Another consideration for those who qualify for higher options levels is the amount of margin used in entering the transaction. The purchase of long stock uses up margin capacity dollar for dollar, whereas the sale of short puts will initially only require approximately 25% of the margin for the same notional position (make sure to check if your short put calls are cash secured or not). A further nuance is whether the position is considered a core holding versus a special situation. If the latter, then the put sale should be favored, whereas if you are looking to potentially hold the position indefinitely, then buying the stock long and selling a call that you are okay with expiring worthless (meaning that you would continue to hold the stock and simply have made incremental portfolio profit from the sale of the call option) is the optimal path. Related, if the company is a dividend payer and you would like to begin to accumulate payouts, then you need to own the stock long to be entitled to future dividend payments.

*If I have sold a put on Company X for $1 and now the option is trading for $0.20, should I buy the option back to lock in a profit, or should I maintain the position?*

In this case the original option trade premise is working, so you should be reluctant to exit this position. As sellers of options, we have time on our side. Most often we are getting paid for waiting patiently. Usually, the sale of a conservative put represents an attempt at hitting a single rather than a home run. All things being equal, it is generally worthwhile to run all the way around the bases. That said, a good rule of thumb is that if you have received 80% or more of the potential profit on a given position (if an option you sold previously is now trading for 20% or less of the original price), and especially if this collapse in options premium has occurred in a short period of time, then you should close out the position. For example, if the option you sold has an expiration date sixty days hence and it is down by 80% or more after only a few weeks from the time you sold the option, then you should consider closing out the position. Another factor that would suggest that you close the naked put would be if the position size is uncomfortably large on a notional basis. In this case, you could close half the position. Furthermore, if your portfolio net long exposure is very high and you are looking to reduce some gross long exposure, short puts that have collapsed in a brief period are good candidates to take off the books as the upside/downside ratio is skewed to losses over gains. In any case, if the underlying fundamentals of the business appear in jeopardy, or if there is a company-specific event like an earnings announcement due between now and expiration, you should look to close out the position as it will possibly go against you, and you have already largely achieved the position's profit potential.

On the call side, if you have sold a call against a long position and the underlying stock price drops (causing the short call option to decrease in price), you might want to consider buying the option back with the goal of reselling the call at a higher price if the stock price rebounds. A scenario in which this might happen is if a stock-specific or macroeconomic event is on the near-term calendar like an earnings report or a Fed meeting. Here are some of the many considerations. Let's say you sold a call on a stock to generate additional income or profit, but you also think the company is a strong one and, unless there is some negative change in the company's fundamentals, you would like to own the stock for the long term. In this case, taking advantage of near-term stock price weakness to buy back the short calls at a profit could be wise because doing so eliminates the possibility that you could be assigned on this quality company. Alternatively, if you are perfectly happy selling the stock at the strike price at which the options are written, then holding the options is worthwhile in order to squeeze out any and all profit opportunities, be they additional options premium decay, stock capital gains, or dividend payment—or some combination thereof.

Generally speaking, don't get too tricky with options once the position is established. For instance, it is difficult to attempt to buy back short call options with the goal of reselling them later at a higher price. Time decay, spreads, and transaction costs are all working against you, especially with near-term options. Stock prices have to move quickly and dramatically to allow you to truly profit from this tactic. Remember, an option trading at $0.50 X $0.60 has a 20% spread; this alone makes the profitable and repeated entry/exit of this derivative security difficult. In most cases, you will not be able to resell the option at a higher price once you have closed it out at a profit. Therefore, let your underlying objectives dictate your actions rather than attempting to time the market or a particular short-term stock price movement. You will get lucky sporadically and nail a stock drop and sudden rebound just right with your short calls, but you will lose more often than you will win. Stick with consistently winning strategies.

*If I purchased a stock and sold ATM calls concurrently, and upon expiration the stock is well below my original purchase price (and thus option strike price), should I sell calls again for nominal premium or wait for stock strength, to try to get more premium later?*

This is a scenario that happens frequently. You buy a given stock and sell ATM or slightly OTM calls, and the long stock position declines so that upon expiration there is little premium in options that expire within ninety days. The question is whether you reach for that nominal premium, sell later-dated options (e.g., 180 days), or wait for stock strength in the hopes that the nearer-dated options will gain premium that you can sell for greater profit. The variables to consider when deciding the optimal tactics include whether the company pays a dividend, what its **beta** is, whether the stock is trading at the low end of its valuation, and what your total portfolio net exposure is, as described in the following figure:

*Figure* **5.7 Variables to Consider for Selling Options**

|  | Yes/High | No/Low |
|---|---|---|
| **Dividends** | Sell Call | Wait |
| **Beta** | Wait | Sell Call |
| **Position of Stock on Valuation Spectrum** | Sell Call | Wait |
| **Portfolio Exposure** | Sell Call | Wait |

The more conservative alternative is to get short premium on the books today. If you end up with a luxury problem, in this case the stock rising above the strike price, then you will have made money in the form of options premium (twice), dividends, and some level of capital gains, depending on how far OTM the original call sale was. This is not a bad outcome. In the other scenario, where the stock does not hit the strike price prior to expiration, you will be glad that you added incremental profits to your portfolio via the short call sale.

*What should I do if a stock I own with covered calls rises and the calls become ATM or ITM?*

The optimal move in this scenario depends on a few variables, including how far OTM the call was when you sold it originally, the time left to expiration, and your objective with the underlying stock. Let's look at these considerations in detail, starting with the two extreme scenarios. In scenario one, assume you bought Company X for short-term trading purposes and sold a far OTM (4% or more) short call option with an expiration date thirty days out. Fast-forward a few weeks and the stock is now trading ATM. In this case, you have captured most of the upside potential associated with this position, having received both the highest capital gain as well as most of the time decay in premium sold. Since the goal was a near-term trade, you are best served by closing this position out since the options provide little downside protection at this point (premium would be very low as expiration is near). With the stock ATM and options expiration just around the corner, the upside associated with the position is very limited, whereas the stock could collapse due to company-specific issues or broad market declines. Be disciplined; the position was entered into as a near-term trade and it worked. Get out and move on to other ideas (or reenter if the stock later declines to a point at which it becomes attractive again).

Examining the other extreme, if you bought Company Y for longer-term investment purposes, sold a near or ATM call to expire in thirty days, and the stock price rises in the near term—as in soon after you purchased it—then you are best served by holding the position since most of the gains associated with this position relate to time decay and only a few days have passed. In this case, your short call premium is still large, and it offers both greater downside protection and time decay profit. If the stock is about to go ex-dividend and your short calls are ITM, that is an extra incentive to hold the position in order to capture both additional option time decay and the dividend.

The guidelines for what to do as an option becomes ATM or ITM are as follows: You should be more inclined to close out the position the more the position is a trade, the closer the option is to expiration, and the farther OTM the original option was. You should be less inclined to sell the more the position is an investment, the farther it is away from expiration, and the closer-to-the-money the option was at time of sale.

For short puts, the optimal time to roll options that are approaching ATM is before the option becomes ITM.

*Do option prices reflect dividends to be paid on the underlying stock? If a company is paying a large special dividend, will options prices be adjusted to reflect the dividend payment?*

In general, options prices reflect the fact that a stock will go ex-dividend between today and expiration. There is no free lunch; it is not as though you get both the benefit of the dividend payment and the entire dividend amount built into the options price (arbitrage situations that arise from time to time are beyond the scope of this book). For example, if you buy Company X stock long on July 3 for $54.20 per share and concurrently sell the July $55 call options, the price in these call options will reflect any dividend payment to be made prior to expiration—or, more precisely, an ex-dividend date prior to expiration as the actual dividend payment might occur later. If the July calls trade for $0.65 per contract, this pricing already reflects a $0.50 dividend payment that you will receive if you hold the stock to the ex-date. Note that if you hold stock long and the short calls become deep ITM approaching an ex-date, often you will be called away (assigned) and will be forced to sell the stock before the ex-date, depriving you of your dividend payment. Keep this in mind when you own stocks long that are covered by ITM calls approaching ex-dates. If you want to continue to own the stock and capture the dividend, you will need to close or roll your call option to either a farther-dated expiration date or a higher strike price (that is OTM), or both. An OTM option will generally not be prematurely assigned and rarely are options that have sixty or more days left until expiration assigned, even if they are fairly ITM.

As for the issue of options adjusting, options chains certainly do get altered to reflect new ticker symbols, stock splits, and the like, but they are only adjusted for special dividends representing 10% or more of the underlying stock price.

If you have sold options on a company that does a spin-off, the option pricing will be adjusted for the spin-off (just as the underlying stock price adjusts) and you may end up with multiple options representing both the original security as well as the spin-off.

Popular ETFs like DIAs and SPYs typically go ex-dividend on the last day of trading before option expiration. Often you will be exercised on ITM short options prior to the ex-date by those who are long the options and want to own the underlying security prior to the ex-date so that they will be paid the dividend. In general, your decision to hold or exercise an option should be driven by your confidence in the underlying security because the stock will drop by the amount of the dividend being paid. Any additional movement in the security will affect your profit.

*Should I sell an entire option position at once, or layer in as I occasionally do with equity positions?*

If your plan is to purchase a stock long and sell a short call against this long position for hedging purposes, you are better served by selling the call at the time you buy the stock long rather than by trying to wait to sell the call on subsequent strength. You might be right on the direction of the stock. Perhaps the stock does go up not long after you buy it and prior to your selling the call. More often, however, time decay will have erased any advantages gained by the increase in stock price, and the premium you get from selling the calls will be less than if you had opened the short call position at the time you purchased the stock long. Remember, as we learned with VIX, rising stock prices tend to correlate with reduced volatility levels, so time decay plus reduced volatility-induced premium loss are all working against you.

Do not confuse this lesson with selling calls on strength in general. The scenario described above is one in which you buy a stock long with the intention of immediately selling calls against that long position to generate additional profits and to hedge your position. A related scenario is using calls to hedge a position that has experienced a material run-up in price. In this latter scenario, you might have bought the stock long at $28 per share with the intention of maintaining the position as a long-term holding and over time the price has increased to the high $30s. Perhaps valuations at this level are frothy, but you still believe in the stock for the long term, so you decide to sell the $40 strike price calls just to provide some near-term hedge. In this case you might hedge only a portion of the position, for example selling five calls on a 1,000-share position. If the stock continues its upward trajectory, then you sell out on half your position at $40 per share plus premium earned with the possibility of repurchasing the shares sold for less than the $40 in the future (or via the sale of five $40 short puts). If the stock retraces prior to expiration, then you have made incremental profit on the short calls that are now worth less than the amount for which you sold them.

If you are layering your long purchases, then by definition you will be selling calls at different times (perhaps even at different strike prices), which is perfectly suitable. For example, if your goal is to purchase a 1,000-share position in Company X but you intend to buy in two tranches if the stock trades lower, you might purchase 500 shares at $27 per share and immediately sell the $27.50 calls. If the stock subsequently falls to $24 per share, you purchase your second lot of 500 shares to dollar cost average down, and in turn sell the $25 calls. Upon expiration, if the stock is trading around $24.50, you might sell the next month's $25 strike price calls on half the position but sell the $27.50s that are ninety days out, the other tranche given insufficient premium in the near dated $27.50 calls. When you have part of a position with room to run (in this case the original 500 shares purchased for $27 per share now trading for $24.50), you can generally sell a tight call on the incremental shares purchased knowing that getting assigned on the lower-priced shares is a good problem to have—since you will still be making money on the shares that are not hedged as tightly. Instead, if you have attained strong premium in your first round of options selling and feel bullish on the stock, you could decide to sell ten of the $27.50 calls for further capital gains potential on the 500 shares for which your effective purchase price is likely around $23 ($24 purchase price less premium collected). This example once again shows the strength and flexibility of options as precise tools to achieve your evolving objectives.

In the case of naked short puts, you can layer them in just like you might layer in stock purchases, acquiring less than a full position at first (via equity purchases in the case of buying stock long, or in the case of naked puts selling, less than a notionally based full position) and adding more contracts if the stock trades lower. That said, because commissions as a percentage of the total position size are so much larger for options than for stocks (which can be $0), and because bid/ask spreads are generally so much wider for options than for stocks, layering in options is not as cost efficient as layering in stocks. Ultimately, the process for layering in is best viewed as a risk control measure more than anything else.

*What moves can I make when naked put options sold are about to expire—either worthless or for potential assignment (ITM)?*

There are a few possible approaches:

1. Let options expire worthless and do not reestablish a position. In this case, the premium collected is your profit. You would take this course of action if your fundamental analysis indicated that the underlying stock on which you sold the put short was no longer a viable investment candidate. You might also choose not to resell options if your total portfolio exposure is such that you are 'overexposed' to stocks. In other words, while you still feel good about the underlying position, your total portfolio exposure could be too net long and you might decide not to sell additional short put exposure so as not to increase incremental long exposure on an already long-biased portfolio. This is smart portfolio risk control.

2. Let options expire worthless and resell new options (either before expiration or post-expiration on the same position—see the section on "doubling up")—either at the same strike price or a lower strike price—to make the position more conservative, depending on where the stock settled at expiration time, VIX levels, and market levels. If you feel bullish on the stock, you would sell the same number of contracts (or more contracts for higher exposure) at the same strike price on a later-dated option. If you are less bullish on the stock, or if your total portfolio composition is such that you do not want this much long exposure, you can sell fewer contracts, or, if the premium allows for it, you can roll down a strike price. For example, if you sold ten puts on Company X with a strike price of $22.50 and the stock closed at $23.10 at expiration, you could either sell fewer contracts at the next-dated $22.50 option (e.g., five, which would halve your notional exposure), or sell ten contracts at the next-dated $20 strike price or some combination thereof. In the latter case, you might have to go out more than one month in order to reduce both notional and delta adjusted exposure this way since selling ten contracts of the $20 strike price puts reduces your notional long exposure to $20,000 from $22,500. In either case, any time you can get a similar amount of premium that you collected from selling the previous short puts by selling a smaller number of new puts or the same number of puts at a lower strike price, you are improving

your risk/reward ratio and this path should be pursued. This is also known as rolling 'down and out.' In this way, you are able to reduce notional and delta adjusted exposure.

3. If the option is in-the-money approaching expiration, you can roll the option to a later-dated expiration for the always sought-after delta premium credit. Note that the deeper ITM the option is, the lower the delta premium credit will be because deep ITM options provide very little time premium (only intrinsic value premium). Furthermore, ITM equity (American-style) options approaching expiration are subject to premature assignment. Thus, if your goal is to keep the short put option, as opposed to close the position entirely or be assigned the stock, you should roll the option as it approaches ATM, and certainly before it gets too deep ITM. In being proactive, you will optimize the delta premium credit you collect and also avoid having to 'take,' or be assigned, the stock.

4. Let option get assigned and hold stock long. If you sold a short put position, you were willing, if not wanting, to own the stock long. In selling an OTM put, you have entered into this position at a lower price than the stock was trading at when you sold the option. In this case, you can hold the stock unhedged as part of your portfolio with the goal of profiting from capital gains and dividends (in the case of a dividend-paying stock). Alternatively, you can immediately sell calls against the assigned stock to profit from options, but this time on the call side rather than the put side. If it is clear you are going to be assigned on or near expiration day (and you qualify), you can presell your calls in anticipation of being assigned. This will allow you to capture additional days' worth of short premium (see the section on "doubling up").

When in doubt, look at your total long exposure (your long stocks, short puts, and long calls) relative to your short exposure, and if you are overexposed on the long side, take your short put profits (either by buying back profitable short puts or by letting them expire without reselling additional puts) as a matter of discipline. If stocks go up, you will make money from your total long exposure. If stocks drop precipitously, you will be glad you did not add incremental long exposure, which you can always add later at a more attractive price.

## LONG OPTIONS TRADING STRATEGIES

The great majority of options expire worthless, just as most insurance policies expire worthless. To be sure, it is always better to be the house; betting against those who control the game and make the rules is generally a loser's game. Selling options, when done intelligently and tactically, can be a great way to hedge, generate income, and add to profits.

What about buying options long? In purchasing options, you have to be accurate in the event, direction, magnitude, and timing. For example, if you purchase an OTM call to expire within thirty days in hopes of profiting from an earnings beat, you have to be right on four counts: that the company exceeds its earnings (the event), that the market reacts in the way you believe it will (the direction), that the subsequent gains are sufficient to cross the break-even hurdle on the OTM purchase (the magnitude), and that this all occurs prior to expiration (the timing). You could be right on two or even three of the four necessary variables and still lose money. Having a call option that was a bet on a pending takeover expire worthless on a Friday only to read on Saturday that a deal was announced after market close (and thus too late) is a painful experience. In certain circumstances long options can provide strong profit or hedging opportunities. Let's examine how to maximize option ownership to your advantage.

If you believe a company represents a good long-term investment opportunity and your goal is to own more of its stock for a long time, you are best served buying ITM long-term options (LEAPS). The deeper in-the-money an option is, the less time value premium there is, most of the premium being intrinsic value premium. With LEAPS, you will get virtually the full benefit of any appreciation in stock price over time while minimizing the negative effects of time decay. In other words, the longer the expiration period and the deeper ITM an option is, the more it behaves like the underlying stock, as delta is near 1.0. The benefit to you of owning ITM options, versus the stock outright, is that you have to shell out less capital to control the same number of shares, and you are paying less for time value premium than if you owned OTM calls.

As an example of an optimal time to use ITM LEAPS for the purchase of an otherwise high-quality company, assume Company X reports weak earnings, sending its stock down 10% or more after the investment banks finish their after-the-fact downgrades. If a trader concludes that the market overreacted, and maintains a long-term bullish position on Company X, but either does not have or chooses not to lay out the capital for buying shares outright (and does not want to hedge via covered calls, given his belief in the strong upside of the stock), the purchase of ITM calls would potentially be a good way to profit. Usually, the sweet spot for buying ITM calls in terms of balancing capital outlays and minimizing time value premium costs is one strike price below where the stock is trading. With the company being quoted at $32 and change after its earnings miss, the in-the-money $30 calls could be a good entry point. How far out should you go timewise? The later-dated options cost more due to more time value premium being embedded in the option, however, they allow for more recovery time for the stock to rebound from its sell-off. A time frame of six to eighteen months, depending on your assessment of how long it will take the company to turn around, is usually a good range to consider (your fundamental analysis will help you determine the appropriate time frame). Figure 5.8 describes an example with associated numbers.

*Figure* **5.8 ITM Long Call Break-Even Analysis**

| Options | Premium | Break-Even Stock Price | % Gain to Break Even |
|---|---|---|---|
| Jan. 2024 Calls; $30 Strike | $4.50 | $34.50 | 7.81% |
| Jan. 2025 Calls; $30 Strike | $5.80 | $35.80 | 11.88% |

Assume Company X stock drops to $32 from $36.40 in the second quarter of 2023. At this point you can either buy the January 2024 $30 strike calls or the January 2025 $30 strikes. To break even on the

2023 contracts, the stock needs to increase to $34.50 (the $30 strike price plus the $4.50 premium). Because the option expires in January 2024, you would have around nine months for the stock to recover at least 7.81% to begin to profit. If you purchase the 2025 January calls, the stock needs to increase 11.88% before you start to profit, however you have around 20 months under this scenario.

When would you want to buy near-term OTM options containing relatively little total premium made up of solely time value premium (no intrinsic value premium)? The time to do this is if you believe a very near-term event such as the announcement of greater-than-expected earnings will move the stock significantly upward prior to the option's expiration date. You must have a specific reason to believe the stock will go up enough to justify the premium paid, otherwise you are merely giving money to the house. Remember, unlike equity ownership, the purchase and sale of options is a zero-sum game of winners and losers. When you lay out cold hard cash for the purchase of an option, you are lining the pocket of someone else on the other side of the transaction. One of you will win, one of you will lose.

*Figure* **5.9 OTM Long Call Break-Even Analysis**

| Options | Premium | Break-Even Stock Price | Required % Gain of Stock |
|---|---|---|---|
| $27.50 strike | $1.15 | $28.65 | 7.91% |
| $30 strike | $0.38 | $30.38 | 14.43% |

As depicted in Figure 5.9, if Company X stock price is at $26.55 and you think that the stock will move upward in the near term, you can buy OTM calls. The likely suspects are either the $27.50 strike or the $30 strike, both expiring about thirty days hence. Buying the $27.50 strike means you are closer to ITM and the stock has a shorter distance to move for you to break even. However, premium on these options is more expensive. If you buy the $30 strike, the stock has farther to increase for you to break even with the premium being lower. In either case, an advantage to buying a call option long rather than buying the stock outright is that your downside is limited to the premium that you have paid for the option. This preset downside limit is an important risk control in and of itself.

## Buying Puts

We have discussed at length the sale of puts. When, if ever, do you want to go long puts? Consistently making money by using puts for market-timing purposes—to bet against the market in the near term—is a difficult undertaking at best. Sure, you may get lucky from time to time but you have decay and general upward market trends working against you. Consequently, you should only go long put premium for three reasons. One, you want to hedge your portfolio at large and are willing to lose the premium to hedge. In this case, you would buy ITM, long-dated options. As discussed, ITM options have a higher delta, thus declines in the broad market will largely be reflected in the price of the put options. You should determine how much of your total portfolio you want to hedge and buy enough options contracts notionally to provide the appropriate hedge. Also, be certain to pick a broad market index that closely resembles your portfolio (e.g., the Russell 2000 if you own mostly small caps, DIAs if you own predominantly large-cap industrials). This is not a market timing bet; it is truly a hedge, a form of portfolio insurance.

A good time to employ this tactic is after a big run-up in the broad markets and a decline in the VIX to low double digits. As with any position, the purchase of a broad-based index put serves a purpose, namely, to protect you against a calamitous event. Thus, if such an event occurs, *be sure to cash in on your insurance policy.* If you total your car, you don't wait until you have a new car to cash in on your policy; you get your totaled car paid for, less the deductible, and you buy insurance again once you are driving a new and safe automobile. So, too, it is important to exercise your long puts once the event you were protecting against happens. That discipline is important, otherwise you are just throwing premiums away. While you will not know when the market has been 'totaled,' you can certainly use your judgment about the value of the long puts and whether they will increase even more in price before expiration. Time is against the option holder, so if stocks drop quickly, causing a dramatic rise in your long put position, consider cashing in. Markets always rebound eventually, and in some cases very quickly, so don't miss your window of opportunity.

Two, you own a specific stock on which you have gains that you want to protect. You have no particular reason to believe that the stock is about to stumble, but you want to buy insurance on this stock to protect your gains. Perhaps the stock represents a large percentage of your portfolio, and you want to hedge against concentration risk while you extend your holding period to gain a tax advantage (a holding period of one year or longer). In this case, the purchase of slightly to moderately OTM long puts is the best course of action as this will provide the direct protection you seek.

Three, contrary to the above example, you have a very specific reason to believe a stock will drop significantly in the near term. Perhaps you think a company will miss earnings or delay a product launch. Long put options give you a low-risk way of profiting from the decline in a stock as your maximum loss exposure is the amount of premium paid. This approach is generally better than shorting the stock, which has unlimited downside potential should you be wrong and the stock goes up instead of down. To determine which strike price to purchase, calculate how large a decline the stock might face, factor in the premium you need to pay in your break-even analysis, and purchase the option accordingly. The key is using options in the right way at the right time, especially when you go long options and time is *not* on your side.

When it comes to put buying, the underlying message is the adage "Do things when you do not have to." The best time to raise money for a company is when the company does not need the money. Call a friend or associate 'just because'—not when you need something from her. Shop around for a new mortgage long before your ARM approaches its fix date. Buy your long puts when everything in life seems good and you have no worries. This is very difficult as the feelings associated with a severe bear market are acute and naturally cause us to want to act whereas when the market is rallying, we just assume that this is the way it is supposed to be, and our guard drops just before the market is about to land an uppercut to the chin. Don't buy fire insurance when you smell the first whiff of smoke: make your purchase during the rainy season when no one is interested in fire protection and rates are cheap. Making a financial move when you *have to* will be more expensive, if not too late, to provide the protection you seek.

Yet most people, especially when it comes to investing, are reactive by nature. While investors' collective memories are short, equities do go through bear markets from time to time, and just as they tend to overshoot on the upside (think 1999–2000 for internet stocks or 2020-2021 for pandemic related 'stay at home' stocks), they have a propensity to undershoot on the downside and last longer than they 'should.' The purchase of a broad-based put option is a great way to protect against the twenty-five-year flood that hits once or twice every decade. Bear markets can be ugly and painful, so if your portfolio has seen good times lately, take out your checkbook and consider buying broad-based stock market disaster insurance so you can sleep well at night. This is especially true if you are approaching the end of your equity-investing time frame (if you need the funds in the next few years) when near-term losses would have an even more damaging effect. It takes tremendous discipline and foresight to buy an umbrella when it is 82 degrees and sunny. But if you own a stock that has gone up a lot in price and you feel compelled to protect against the downside, buy puts *then*. Take a step back and realize that a storm could be just around the corner. Buy your insurance early, and on the cheap.

## THE OPTIMAL TIME TO SELL PUTS

As we have learned, it is almost always better to be the house—to be the seller of insurance. But when is the optimal time to be the seller of put premium? *When everyone is scared of the event they are trying to protect against and premiums are high.* When people are willing to bid up the price of insurance for what is still a highly unlikely event to unreasonable levels, that is when you want to sell as much of the stuff as you can within your risk control parameters. You still need to do your fundamental research on a given company combined with a wise dose of macroeconomic and technical analysis.

Periodically an otherwise great company experiences a short-term, nonfundamental problem, the stock drops, the investment banks lower their price targets, and only once the stock has already gone down do people typically rush in to buy puts, thus bidding up the price of this insurance dramatically both in terms of directional and volatility-induced enhanced premiums. When there is blood in the stock market waters, that is when you will find the best put selling opportunities, especially for your special situation positions. Fortunately, the stock market is a large and diverse and thus there are often many opportunities to take advantage of people's overreactions based on emotional responses to events—and to happily accept the premiums that they are willing to pay for what will likely end up worthless to them and highly profitable for you. Most fear-and greed-driven trends tend to last longer than most investors expect them to. But, if you do your homework, you should eventually be proven right and be richer for it.

## Key Takeaways:

- You can sell puts to replace stock that is about to be assigned from covered calls.
- Depending on your goals and risk profile, you can optimize the mix of potential price appreciation, dividends, and options premium income to suit your circumstances.
- When in doubt, do the conservative thing of taking profits on options, especially if you hold naked calls, as a profitable position can turn negative quickly if you get caught short stock with naked calls.
- Only sell puts at a level (notional exposure) where you can comfortably take ownership of the stock. Don't sell so many contracts that being assigned would mean you would go deep into margin or have an excessively large position size.
- Long calls can be used for speculation or stock replacement. Long puts can be used for specific position hedges, to speculate on broad market movements, or to protect your portfolio from sudden sell offs.

# CHAPTER 6

## CONSTRUCTING A PORTFOLIO: RISK CONTROLS, IDEA GENERATION, POSITION SIZING, AND OTHER RELEVANT PARAMETERS

We hate losing money. Actually, take that back; hate is a pretty strong word. Hate *hate hate hate* to lose money would be a more accurate way of putting it. However, in order to attain real investment returns, you must take on some level of risk and be subject to short-term declines. In the immortal words of Thomas Crown, "Do you want to dance or do you want to *dance?*" Similarly, there are losses and then there are *losses;* there are mistakes and then there are *mistakes.* Knowing the difference, and using smart risk control to avoid the latter, will put you on the path to superior investment returns over time. Thinking you are immune to the 100-year flood that invariably arrives every few years may put your portfolio permanently underwater.

In this chapter we focus on how to properly construct a portfolio. It is one thing to be able to pick good stocks. It is another thing entirely to build and manage a portfolio that will provide superior returns over time. When you assemble a collection of largely dividend-paying securities, coupled with effective options strategies, you can end up with a portfolio that not only credits your account consistently and regularly with dividend payments and premium sales, but also has the potential to provide consistently superior returns. Let us examine in more detail how this is accomplished.

## RISK: DEFINITIONS AND CONTROLS

Anything worthwhile in life involves taking some level of risk relative to the potential reward. Want to run a marathon? You risk getting injured. Want to find that perfect person? You risk getting your heart ripped out.

Want to get into an Ivy League school? You risk being rejected. Risk is one of the most important considerations in portfolio construction. Yet risk is also one of the most misunderstood—if not misused—concepts in money management.

The definition of risk that you hear used regularly by brokerage firms, market commentators, and financial advisors relates to volatility: how much a given investment is likely to go up or down over a certain period, usually between a few days and twelve months at the long end. In fact, how much someone can stomach the ups and downs of the market is often the dominant consideration for investment professionals attempting to determine how to construct client portfolios. Every day, all across America, financial advisors ask a series of questions aimed largely at determining a client's comfort level with risk as defined by volatility. But is this really the best definition of investment risk? Is it even a good one? A useful one?

Imagine a personal trainer having an initial conversation with a client whose goal is to lose thirty pounds over the next twelve months:

"So, you want to lose thirty pounds by this time next year? That is an excellent long-term physical goal. I think I can help you a lot in achieving this objective. I just have a couple questions for you. First, do you weigh yourself regularly?"

"Yes."

"Okay, how do you feel about weighing yourself—do you like doing this?"

"No, I hate weighing myself."

"Would you say that it is emotionally challenging to see your weight going up and down?"

"Absolutely. That is why I hate weighing myself!"

"Okay, then," declares the trainer. "We will adjust your training program accordingly."

No! This is exactly the wrong issue on which to focus; it is letting the tail wag the dog. In the case of portfolio construction, why let an emotional aversion be the dominant factor in constructing a plan that must be rigorous and objective to succeed? This is, in effect, the outcome for many investors who are unable to overcome their emotions—and for advisors who are unable or unwilling to do the hard work necessary to educate investors and convince them to do what is right for their pocketbooks, not what feels the most comfortable. Just as the effective personal trainer should counsel his client to only weigh herself every month or so to check the progress toward her twelve-month goal, and to focus instead on the important elements of the plan (consistency in workouts, quality diet, etc.), so too should the professional money manager guide his clients away from checking stock prices at frequencies inconsistent with their investment time horizon. And certainly, the advisor should not alter the plan to cater to the nervousness of the client by, for example, over-allocating bonds to smooth out the ride at the potential cost of ending up at the destination with less money to spend.

Daily headline noise should be the last thing driving the portfolio construction process. Rather, the first line of discussion should relate to time frames associated with the investor's financial objective. The goal of investing is to allocate X amount of capital today in order to have X + Y capital at a future date. If the money is intended for retirement, for example, and the investor is in her early forties, what happens today, tomorrow, next week, next month, or even next year is irrelevant—just as, with our slightly overweight friend who wants to lose thirty pounds over the next twelve months, day-to-day weight fluctuations should not be the focal point. To be sure, results and progress should be reviewed from time to time, but at reasonable intervals relative to the goal, and with the focus on processes and inputs.

**POWER TIP**

**The Ticker Gave In**

Imagine if the day after you moved into your new home, a house you planned to sell in the distant future, the abode 'went public' and you could track its current price no differently than you can track stocks. UP $10,000! DOWN $13,000! In addition to having access to minute-by-minute vacillations of the price (not value, mind you, but price), you also have the privilege of continuous broadcasts telling you with authority the causes for yesterday's gain or loss. "Your house lost $18,000 yesterday because your neighbor's kids left their toys out on the front porch thus causing broad losses throughout the block." All this useless input and after-the-fact analysis would drive you crazy. Even though your heart is where your home is, you would quickly 'de-list' your house so that you would no longer be subject to monthly, weekly, daily, and even hourly price quotes. In doing so, you would live in peace knowing that you had bought a quality home in a good neighborhood at a reasonable price. Five or ten years hence—perhaps a year or so before you intended to sell—you would begin to check the market and see how your home is priced. But in the meantime, you would not pay attention to near-term price fluctuations.

Since we know that short-term volatility is not an adequate characterization of risk, let us examine some true sources of portfolio peril.

### Risk Comes from Not Knowing What You Are Doing

This is the best definition of risk. Is a scalpel risky? In the hands of a toddler, yes. In the palm of an experienced surgeon, it is a potential lifesaver. How about being dropped a mile offshore in the ocean? To the person who never learned to swim, this situation is full of risks. To the athlete training to swim the English Channel, his downside risk (not making it to shore safely) is very small given his skill set. Indeed, to build his endurance and achieve his objective, he *has* to undertake such activities. Relative to his objectives, *not* placing himself a mile offshore—not training appropriately—is risky. In practically every situation, the risk we take is a function of our skill sets. Risk is rarely an absolute; it is almost never the same for everyone, given individuals' different competencies, mental makeups, physical abilities, and so on.

When it comes to investing, people take risks every day that relate quite simply to their not knowing what they are doing, to their not being adequately informed. Why? Because it is so easy to do. The barriers to entry are low and access to information via sources like the Internet is easier than ever. This reality makes the stock market less efficient in the short term, not more efficient as many had predicted. The theory that the market would become ultra-efficient as more and more people started investing and trading on their own behalf assumed that the players in the market would act rationally and use the complete information available. This has not been the case. Time and time again, investors buy stocks based solely on a tip, or on the fact that they saw the price go up recently, or because they heard the name mentioned on a financial show. And is the disposition of stock always based on the latest and most comprehensive information available on a given company? Certainly not. Sometimes an investor sells because he needs the money for that month's mortgage payment! The average investor chases returns, buying more when the market is up and less when the market is down. The average investor also does not know what he is investing in; he has not researched the fundamentals of the underlying business. Thus, it is not surprising that studies indicate the average investor's returns over the last twenty to thirty years have been about one-third of what the market has returned over that time.

All other risks are essentially a subset of this first risk. If you know what you are doing, you will likely not make the other mistakes that are the main source of investment risk.

## *Risk Comes from Not (Truly) Knowing Anything About the Companies You Are Buying*

Think of the classic scene in a movie in which a man, having unknowingly slept with a mobster's wife, is then informed by a friend that he is dead but doesn't even know it yet. When you buy the stock of a company you know little to nothing about, you may be financially dead and not even know it yet. Or to paint a less gruesome picture, you are like one of those cartoon characters who has been chased off the edge of a cliff; your feet are still moving but the next direction is straight down. You might get lucky and the stock might work out, but relying on luck or hope or tips for investment profits is a way to ensure inferior returns if not permanent capital losses. Without question, the elimination of your three biggest mistakes/losses in a given year—primarily through the discipline of taking no action—will add more profit to your portfolio than your three biggest winners will.

Many people 'playing' the market buy stocks based on a ticker symbol or a slick software package that is flashing green or red, up or down, rather than on thorough company analysis. Rarely do they know *what* they are buying. Basing investment decisions solely on price is like saying yes when someone asks you if you would like to buy water for $1 and not knowing whether the water is a gallon of Evian's finest or an ounce of polluted, disease-filled river water. The price per share tells you nothing about the company, its total enterprise value, its true worth, or its competitive position. Yet many investors use this as their main, if not sole, source of information when it comes to investing, often looking in the rearview mirror and assuming that if the stock has been ticking upward it will continue to do so regardless of valuation, or that because the stock was once trading for $20 and is now selling for $12, it *must* be a bargain. Conversely, investors will often hold on to a $25 stock as it becomes a teenager because they psychologically want to sell it once it gets back to breakeven, their anchor price, regardless of what the company is truly worth. If you do not sincerely comprehend the underlying fundamentals of the companies to which you are allocating capital, then you are taking real risks that have nothing to do with the daily ups and downs of the market but will likely have a real impact on your account balance over time.

Bottom line, if you do not have the time and inclination to dedicate the resources necessary to increase your probability of success, stick to broad-based indices that will minimize any material downside—or else find someone you trust who manages money professionally on a full-time basis.

**POWER TIP**
**There Are Losses and There Are Losses**

As the Oracle himself, Warren Buffett, has said many times when it comes to investing: *Rule #1: Don't lose money. Rule #2: Don't forget Rule #1.* But many people misinterpret this message and pay the long-term price of inferior investment returns for the error. Buffett is specifically *not* saying don't lose money *ever.* On the contrary, he is also quoted as saying you should be prepared to lose as much as 50% on a given stock post-purchase. How do you reconcile these seemingly contradictory concepts?

The answer is subtle and simple, but powerful. When Buffett says don't lose money, he is referring to *permanent capital losses.* He is saying, in effect, do not make stupid investments in the stocks of low-quality companies that you know nothing about and that might see their price go to zero... permanently. But having the stock of a quality company go down 30%, 40%, 50% due to uncontrollable market forces before heading back north to the land of profits? No problem. None other than AMZN and other great companies have seen their stock prices drop 50% or more multiple times on the road to investor riches.

If experiencing a temporary decline in stock prices is not considered an investment mistake, what breaches of investing discipline should we be avoiding in order to improve portfolio returns? Here are some additional common mistakes that can truly have a permanent negative impact on your portfolio.

*Risk Comes from Mismatching the Time Frame Associated with Your Investment Objective and the Type of Investment You Are Using to Achieve This Objective*

As the saying goes, time heals all wounds. When it comes to investing, time is on your side—if you manage it correctly.

Cash is one of the least risky investments, right? You will hear again and again that if you want to avoid risk, you should put your money in a stable money market fund for example, as it is virtually assured of maintaining its 1.0 net asset value. Again, this places the emphasis on volatility. What if your goal is to save for the college tuition you antici-pate coming due in twelve years? If you had the choice between putting $10,000 in a money market fund and investing the same $10,000 into the S&P 500, which would be riskier? Looking at this scenario in terms of the investment objective and time horizon—which is how risk should be measured—putting the $10,000 in a money market fund is by far the riskier bet, as the money will likely be worth about the same if not less on a real, post-inflation basis twelve years from now (especially given that higher education prices have risen 5% - 6% per year on average for years).

Compare this outcome with that of putting the funds in the S&P 500. Will that index see large declines from time to time over the sub-sequent twelve years? You bet. There is a great probability that the index will periodically drop 10% or more from peak to trough given the index's historical **standard deviation** of approximately 15%. But, given the twelve-year time horizon, this volatility is essentially mean-ingless. Interim ups and downs only matter if you need the money in the interim. The difference between earning 3% or 4% in cash and 7% - 9% average annual returns in equities over 10+ years is dramatic and can make the difference between being able to afford college or not. Match your investments to your time horizon and volatility becomes your friend (remember, too, if you own dividend-paying stocks, you will naturally dollar cost average down when prices decline. To the extent you own companies that are repurchasing their own shares, price declines also work in your favor over time).

If we could garner only one piece of information from a new client, it would not be the misapplied concept of 'risk tolerance.' It would be the simple question of: *When do you need the money back*? One year? No problem, we'll invest accordingly. Ten years? That requires a differ-ent portfolio entirely.

Many investors track their long-term holdings on a monthly, weekly, or even daily basis. The media does not help matters by pre-senting investing and financial news as though it were a terrorist alert.

One financial news show has even displayed a countdown clock to when the U.S. markets closed that showed how much time was left on the clock to the *hundredth of a second!* Investing in stocks should be more akin to running a marathon than a sprint.

## Risk Comes from Taking on Too Much Leverage

Every few years, like clockwork, a high-profile hedge fund or major financial institution blows up. What are the two most common themes in these meltdowns? You can bet one of them related to leverage. The more leverage you take on, the smaller your margin for error—and the less you can withstand temporary fluctuations in portfolio values that otherwise would pose no problem. Take $1,000 to Vegas and if you end up down 10%, you walk away with $900. Not a great outcome, but not devastating enough to ruin your weekend. Take the same $1,000, leverage it up 10× with the house's 'easy' money so that you now have $10,000. Lose a few bets so that you are down 10% and your entire capital, the $1,000 with which you came to Vegas, is obliterated. A 20% loss at that level of leverage wipes out your capital and leaves you in hock to boot. That is the destructive power of leverage.

If used correctly—if the cost of the leverage is low and, more important, if the holding time horizon is sufficient to ride out the inevitable ups and downs, and if the user of the leverage is not beholden to the supplier of the leverage for continued access to that capital in good times and bad—then leverage can be a productive source of return enhancement. Leverage is the essence of the United States real estate mortgage industry. However, even those industry dynamics changed with real estate 'investors' taking out short-term loans, putting little or no money down (read: higher than historical leverage; the difference between 20% down and 5% down can easily mean the difference between riding out the storm and foreclosure), and looking to make near-term gains by flipping houses (read: speculating rather than investing). This short-term, highly leveraged game works as long as the music is playing, but as soon as it stops, the 'house' wins and you lose, with leverage magnifying the damages.

## *Risk Comes from Attempting to Short a Company or the Market as a Whole Without Proper Expertise*

Shorting stock—borrowing it, selling it, and hoping it goes down so that you can repurchase it at a lower price and pocket the difference in profits—is a dangerous game. Undoubtedly, the shorts have their day in the rain from time to time, but the financial odds are stacked against them. Stocks go up over time, so right off the bat you have the long-term trend working against you. To short stocks means borrowing costs. Strike two. Your upside is limited (a stock price cannot become negative) whereas the downside is unlimited (you could have shorted Google at its seemingly overvalued IPO price and the stock might never see that level again). Strike three.

Shorting the market at large is a form of market gambling. Occasionally you will be right; in most cases you will be wrong. If your investments match your time frame, then the fact that the market goes down in the interim is irrelevant. Do not try to be too tricky and short the market. Losing money when the market is going up—experiencing permanent capital losses—is a financial sin. Own a quality dividend-paying company, and if the market and the stock price of this company go down, no big deal—you can collect the dividend check and reinvest it; you don't need the capital today anyway. Let the long-term market, economic, and financial forces work in your favor for long-term gains. Betting against a quality company based solely on valuation, or on the market at large, is a loser's game.

Shorting should be left to people who dedicate their professional lives to finding specific companies that are likely to go to zero due to scam situations or dramatically deteriorating financial fundamentals—the very things you need to avoid on the long side (indeed the shorts are *selling* stock to *you*). If you have some very specific and in-depth information about a company and why it is likely to see a material decline in its operations, perhaps you should consider dedicating a small amount of capital to shorting the stock. Or, for a more broad-based hedge, you can short an index ETF and hedge the short by creating a sell write. Like any position, this should not represent more than about 5% of your total portfolio. Bottom line, shorting equities is a full-time job, not something to play around with in your spare time. Otherwise, you may soon be asking people if they can spare some change.

## Risk Comes from Lack of Liquidity

The other common theme in financial blowups is that of liquidity, specifically the lack thereof. When you sell because you have to rather than because you want to, you sell from a position of weakness. When the market for the given investment has dried up, you will likely take a beating. Certain assets are inherently less liquid than others. Golf courses are harder to sell than shares of IBM. There are fewer potential buyers and thus, if the market is turning south, the law of supply and demand works against you. Often integrally related to the risk of lack of liquidity is the risk of concentration. If a good chunk of your portfolio is in that golf course and you need to raise cash, you have few options in what to liquidate and those on the other side of the transaction will use that to their advantage.

In these scenarios, if the market is heading in your favor, then the inherent risks are masked. During the rainy season, you don't notice the risk of your house catching on fire. It is when the downside comes that true risks are exposed. The key is to remember that the weather will turn hot and dry eventually and to act before it is too late. Protect yourself against worst-case scenarios and the permanent loss of capital by not over-leveraging and having an overly concentrated portfolio.

## Risk Comes from Overpaying for a Good Company or, Worse, Buying a Bad Company

Remember, unless you are a professional investor with a mandate of always being fully invested, you don't have to put every last long-term investment dollar into stocks. It does not occur often, but from time to time the overall market or particular segments can have excessive valuations. Examples include internet stocks in the late 1990s, and newfangled technology companies around 2020/2021 that were trading at 50X+ sales. Using a more mundane example of KO, if you purchased this company in 1999, your returns for the following 10 years were as flat as a four-day old open can of coke. KO was a great company in

1999, but a bad stock due to its excessive valuation. At least with KO you earned over 40 dividend payments from 1999 – 2009 and reinvested many of those at lower prices for natural dollar cost averaging. Don't forget that the reinvestment of dividends is one of the most important parts of wealth creation over time. While returns were not that attractive, with this high-quality company you were close to keeping up with inflation after factoring in dividends paid. This is an example of overpaying for a good company.

Compare this with buying a second-rate company with no earnings trading at 50X+ *sales* some Web 3.0-type companies were in the 2020/2021 time frame. A number of such companies are down 70% - 80% or more from their peaks, and it could be decades if ever before they return to prior highs. No dividends are being paid out in the interim, thus no dollar cost averaging is taking place, further lengthening the runway to recouped losses. Several third-tier companies went bankrupt or continue to struggle for survival.

While most investors should have a strong value orientation for core holdings, always looking for high-quality companies at reasonable prices, you would rather make the mistake of over-paying for a quality company than buying a bad company that might experience permanent capital loss. In the case of Coca-Cola, while you were waiting patiently for the company's earnings to catch up to its valuation (and, indeed, Coke was earning nearly triple per share in the late '00s versus what it earned ten years prior), you were getting paid an ever-increasing dividend that was being reinvested at lower and lower prices.

When stocks are expensive, the probability of superior future returns is lowered dramatically. Avoid making the mistake of overpaying, even for a high-quality company. If you are patient, you will be surprised how often high-quality companies go on sale. As the saying goes, the market takes an escalator up and an elevator down. Wait near the first floor with a barrel full of cash and step in when the elevator door opens full of great companies on sale.

### Risk Comes from Not Knowing Who Your Money Manager Is

If one were to ask 100 otherwise intelligent people with decent-sized portfolios who is the person making investment decisions on their behalf, who is the one deciding how their hard-earned money is allocated, the vast majority could not name that person. Of those who know that some often-in-the-press money manager is the one pulling the trigger for their mutual fund, only a few will ever have met this person, had an in-depth conversation with him or her, or discussed goals, objectives, and time horizons. Those who have money with the big brokerage firms have typically only met their 'financial consultant,' who is often nothing more than a salesperson. These folks do not make investment decisions on their clients' behalf. The actual money manager is typically several layers away operationally and geographically far removed from the client. Imagine never getting to meet the person making important decisions for you in law or medicine. Would you find it comforting, not to mention effective, if your child's pediatrist lived 3,000 miles away and never interacted directly with you or your child? Most investors should be concerned about the fact that they do not even know the name of, let alone anything else about, the person managing their hard-earned money. Without regular, direct contact between the client and the money manager, how can objectives be monitored and updated? How can changing circumstances (a new child or a new job) be factored into the investment plan? Get to know the person making decisions about your financial future and reduce the risk associated with the lack of a relationship between client and money manager.

People over-attribute risk to market elements beyond their control and underestimate the risk associated with factors within their purview, namely their own actions and behaviors. At the end of the day, risk is not volatility, as it is traditionally defined in the stock market, rather it is not knowing what you are doing; making investment decisions based on emotion rather than hard facts; over-leveraging; paying too high a price for your investments or, worse yet, purchasing bad companies; and being overly concentrated.

Now that we have a better handle on risk and how it relates to portfolio construction, let us look at some specifics in terms of how to use equities and options in creating a portfolio that can tap into the power and magic of compounding.

## PORTFOLIO CONSTRUCTION

The investing and trading style espoused in this book can be characterized as disciplined and value-hedged. Consistency and self-control are
keys to superior performance and long-term success. As noted in several
sections of this book, deviating from your investing and trading strategy—from your predefined rules—even for a short time to squeeze out
a few extra dollars of profits, is a surefire way to incur losses that will be
difficult to recover within a reasonable time frame. The superior investor must know more than how to pick a great company, as a single stock
does not a portfolio make. Rather, one must know how to continually
generate good investment ideas, how to enter and build positions, how
and when to sell, how and when to hedge—and how many positions
to hold and in what proportions. In this section we discuss these vital
elements from start to finish.

### Idea Generation

Where are good sources of investing and trading ideas? Good resources
for equity possibilities and analysis (macro, industry, company) are
largely as follows:

- General observation: having an investor perspective in life,
  listening to people and conducting commerce.
- Company annual reports, 10-Ks, earnings releases, conference
  calls, and other company-specific information.
- News sources, such the *Wall Street Journal, Barron's,* and the
  *New York Times.* Industry periodicals.
- Colleagues whose views we trust (not for stock picks, but for
  informative discussions).
- Value Line (an objective company information source).
- Standard & Poor's (an objective company information source).
- Argus (an objective company information source).
- A few investment bank research groups (to check in with their
  thinking; they are often contrarian indicators).

One source noticeably absent from the above list is the financial talk shows that have become extremely popular. The fact is that doing the hard work is time-consuming and difficult, which is why most people don't do it. Listening to someone take three seconds on TV to talk about a stock is useless at best. When these commentators are asked if they own what they have just screamed that everyone is crazy not to own, nine out of ten times they answer "no." Remember, commentators are paid to commentate (or entertain), not to manage your portfolio.

## Core Holdings and Special Situations

Having identified good idea sources, you must next predefine your criteria for equity selection. That way you will know quickly whether a company that comes across your radar screen is even a candidate for consideration. One effective way to do this is to put your stocks into two separate buckets, **core holdings** and **special situations**. Core holdings should consist of quality dividend-paying companies that meet your valuation metrics and dividend payout ratios. These are typically intended to be longer-term holdings that you either hedge via short calls or hold long unhedged to take advantage of potential capital gains and dividend reinvestment.

Special situation stocks can be defined as companies that pay little or no dividends but that are otherwise quality companies that, temporarily and for nonfundamental reasons, have fallen on hard times. Special situation stocks tend to be shorter-term trade-oriented, often with the goal of taking advantage of a spike in put premium associated with a quick drop in the stock. Special situation stocks are often bad news stocks or sectors (by industry or geography). Think about tracking a few dozen companies and ETFs and, if on a given day one of them drops dramatically, or meets some predetermined price threshold, consider attaining exposure (e.g., via the sale of short puts). Whenever there is bad news, pay attention as put premiums have inevitably been bid up and opportunities abound.

Mergers are a good example of special situations and a good, understandable representation of **arbitrage**. At its essence, arbitrage is the taking advantage of discrepancies based on either distance or price or both. Today, price arbitrage is more common when the bid for a security differs even infinitesimally from one market to another. These discrepancies are increasingly more difficult to capture given advances in technology. But in the case of merger arbitrage, such gaps between price arise, in this case the dimension being that of time. Often there is uncertainty associated with whether a given takeover will occur. Consequently, the premium in the puts can be quite large. As an example, assume Company X is in the process of being taken over. The expected take-out price is $33 per share, however, the market is uncertain as to whether or not the transaction will take place, and thus the stock trades in the $26 to $31 range for several months. The premium associated with the $25 strike price puts could remain unusually large for a very long time period.

**Figure 6.1 Enhanced Put Premiums Associated with Merger Arbitrage**

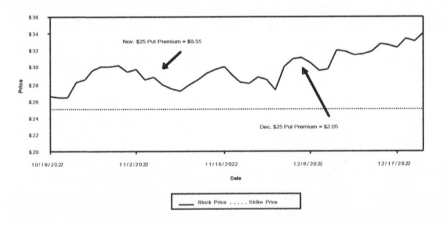

SOURCE: MARKETDATAEXPRESS.COM

Of course, if the deal does not get consummated, the stock will likely trade down to its pre-takeover levels, so you need to be willing to own the stock at the strike price at which you are selling the puts. You can always hedge your short put position by buying farther out-of-the-money long puts at the next strike price. As discussed in the options section, such a position limits downside risk to the spread between the two strike prices. Merger arbitrage is a field unto itself, so tread carefully if you are using takeovers as a source of profitability. Special situation stocks tend to be smaller positions, in the 2% to 4% range on a notional basis in terms of short put exposure.

**POWER TIP**

**She's Got Legs (So Know How to Use Them)**

Like a shark, we are attracted to blood in the water that represents an otherwise quality company that has been beaten down. Learn from mistakes, however, and refrain from entering a position the day that bad news is released. While a stock that has fallen will occasionally rebound quickly, that is the exception. The first thing to occur after a company's stock falls is that most of the investment banks issue downgrades, adding further selling pressure to the stock. Then, the big mutual funds that have mandates to sell any stock that misses its earnings begin their drawn-out selling process. Finally, a bottom will form days or even weeks after the event that led to the decline. To be sure, the stock's volatility will be at its peak on the days following the negative event. But this is one of the few times when putting premium on the books (assuming the position is entered into via farther OTM short puts) is often best done only after the dust settles. This is so you can be certain that there is no more bad news (which is not an uncommon phenomenon for truly broken companies—first they crack, then they crumble). The benefits to avoiding such an outcome greatly outweigh missing a few points of premium were you to act upon the release of the bad news.

## To Hedge or Not to Hedge, That Is the Question

How much hedging you employ is largely driven by your investment objectives and time frames. The shorter the investment time horizon, the more an investor should hedge her portfolio, and the tighter the

**POWER TIP**
**Returning That Special Delivery**

If you have taken a position—either via direct equity ownership or by way of the sale of a short put—in a special situation stock that is not a core holding, consider employing a tight stop-loss sell discipline of 10% or less.

hedges should be. All things being equal, call options sold should be closer to ATM, as opposed to far OTM. The longer one's investment horizon, the less hedged a portfolio should be. If you are in your forties and managing a retirement account, hedging should be done very selectively. (Remember, the sale of calls is first and foremost a profit generating trading technique; it can certainly be used appropriately within the context of longer-time-horizon accounts, but it must be employed more discerningly). This retirement account has a very long time horizon, and one potential downside in selling calls that are too tight, or sold on weakness rather than strength, is that the upside potential associated with equity appreciation can be curtailed if one is too aggressive with call sales. On the investment objective side, the more growth-oriented an account is, the less hedging should be employed, whereas an income orientation is well suited for dividend-focused stocks coupled with option sales. Depending on stock and volatility levels, you can often generate 1.5X to 3X in options premium over what is paid in the form of a dividend. For example, if you buy Company X that pays a 3% dividend, you can reasonably generate another 4.5% to 9% of incremental income annually through the sale of options, especially ATM. During high VIX environments the amount of income available from options sales can be even higher. In short, you can certainly create a portfolio with superior return potential that is absent of options—for example, a long-term portfolio such as a child's 529 college savings plan, which needs little incremental trading in order to achieve its objectives. But for appropriate accounts and for those willing to dedicate the time to learn and monitor positions accordingly, the use of options on top of dividend-paying stocks can be thought of as equities on steroids.

*Figure* **6.2 Hedging Strategies Associated with Investment Objectives**

|  | Growth | Income |
|---|---|---|
| **Long Time Horizon** | Little to No Hedging | Moderate Hedging |
| **Short Time Horizon** | Moderate Hedging | Most Hedging |

A final consideration for the level of options selling that you should include in your portfolio is that of stock valuations. If the market has taken a beating so that P/E ratios are on the low end of the historical range, you should hedge less—regardless of time horizon and investment objective. The sale of a call is a form of a short, and depressed markets are a time to buy, not sell. (This would be a good time to enhance returns via more aggressive put sales, especially given that a depressed market is typically associated with a high VIX and thus rich put premium levels). Conversely, if the market as a whole, or a single stock holding in your portfolio, has risen so that the valuation is flush—although not so much that you want to exit the position—the sale of a call can provide some near-term downside protection, and in the case of an assignment, it will 'force' you to sell when the stock is trading at a premium. In many cases, the stock price will retrace and you will have the opportunity to repurchase the stock at a lower price post-assignment.

## ETFs Versus Mutual Funds

Let's discuss mutual funds as a vehicle for investing and trading. For the small accounts of passive investors, a low-cost mutual fund can be an excellent vehicle for wealth creation over time. The same holds true for

**POWER TIP**

**Fire and Rain (Keeping Your Gunpowder Dry)**

Maintaining at least some cash level, or available equity-buying power, along with a 'wish list' of stocks that you would like to buy if prices become attractive enough is an excellent way to create wealth. A cash level of 10% of your total portfolio represents a good starting point. When things get ugly, selling begets selling, and often quality companies see their stock prices cut to unreasonably cheap levels. This is when you want to be the buyer, not the seller. These opportunities might not present themselves for years, but when they do you need to have the ammunition necessary to shoot the fish in the barrel. Maintain the discipline of having your target list and the means to buy them at fire-sale prices.

When people need to raise cash, they will sell at virtually any price. That is where you step in. Remember, since your portfolio likely has exposure beyond your long stocks by way of short puts and short calls, even though you have 10% of your capital in the form of cash, your total portfolio exposure may well exceed 100%. This is another advantage of using options in your portfolio; it allows you to maintain high levels of exposure to the market while keeping your gunpowder dry for future opportunities.

the investor who is adding small amounts to his account at regular intervals. Most mutual funds will let you purchase additional shares in very small increments without sales charges; thus, for those putting money away monthly from their paycheck, for example, mutual funds can be a good investment vehicle. By definition, a set monthly investment achieves dollar-cost averaging—buying more shares when the market is down and fewer shares when the market is high—and maintaining this disciplined approach is important. Too many people turn off their automatic investment plans just when they should be increasing them, namely when the market is down. He who buys at the lowest price wins, so you are *always* better off putting money to work when broad indices are down rather than when they are up. Don't fall prey to novice investor mistake *numero uno,* which is to buy high and sell low. Start a plan, focus on keeping costs low, and stick to it. That is the very best way you can tap into the power of compounding.

Mutual funds, however, have certain inherent disadvantages over ETFs and individual stocks. The first is that of liquidity (frequency of trading). While for investors with very long time horizons, intra-day trading is not essential, for traders looking to take advantage of near-term fluctuations, the once-a-day pricing of mutual funds represents a negative. By contrast, ETFs trade throughout the market day. And even if you are not concerned about trading a fund intra-day, you could be discouraged to have entered your mutual fund order in the morning when the market was up, only to discover when you confirm the sale order the next day that your price was much lower than expected because the broad market sold off late in the day. Furthermore, the portfolio holdings of mutual funds are stale, with position updates quarterly at best. The fund manager could have made material changes to the portfolio between the time the holdings were last published and the time you bought into the fund, so you cannot be certain what you are buying. ETFs, on the other hand, often have essentially fixed portfolios, the contents of which are available for review and analysis at any point. You know more and you have more control over what you are buying.

Another advantage of ETFs is that they can be sold short; you can bet that they will decline in value. This adds additional flexibility in terms of risk control and portfolio management. ETFs tend to be more cost effective; actively managed mutual funds can have expense ratios of 1% or more, versus an expense ratio of around 0.05% - 0.3% for most ETFs. Taxes are another reason to choose ETFs over mutual funds, the latter often paying out large capital gains even to those who did not participate in the earnings themselves. Getting the tax status on mutual fund holdings is often challenging, which can lead to nasty surprises and large tax bills for those who buy into a given fund just prior to distributions (these usually occur toward the end of the year). ETFs, on the other hand, do not typically have any embedded taxable gains.

The final important factor when considering ETFs versus their mutual fund cousins is the ability to sell options against the underlying securities. Simply put, there are no options on mutual funds. There is no way to directly hedge or take advantage of your mutual fund's holdings by generating income through call sales, for example. By contrast, many hundreds of ETFs have options that trade against them.

Bottom line, for sophisticated investors, ETFs and individual stocks are superior to mutual funds when it comes to structuring and hedging a portfolio.

*Figure* **6.3 Advantages of ETFs over Mutual Funds**

| ETFs | Mutual Funds |
|---|---|
| Trade throughout the day | Trade 1× per day |
| Have lower costs | Often have higher costs |
| Able to short | Cannot short |
| Can sell options against | Cannot sell options against |
| Real-time holdings known | Stale portfolio info—as much as six months old |
| Tax efficient | Can be very tax inefficient |
| Not adversely affected by fund flows | Affected by fund flows as big capital infusions force the manager to buy more stocks. Similarly, big withdrawals force the manager to sell stocks, causing adverse tax consequences as other investors are forced to cover the fixed expenses |
| Portfolios typically fixed | Managers often buy 'hot stocks' at the end of the quarter, dump their losers just to 'markup' their books to look better in the eyes of investors—chasing after 'winners' for appearances only |

## Portfolio Size: Using Individual Stocks Versus ETFs

Whether to use individual stocks as opposed to ETFs depends on several variables. The first factor is portfolio size. Diversification within your portfolio is important, and while a low-six-figure portfolio size is a good starting point for the use of individual securities to achieve return objectives, it is difficult to get adequate diversification using individual stocks if a portfolio is under $100,000 in total value. A portfolio of under $100,000 should contain primarily ETFs in order to get equity exposure. Fortunately, there are hundreds of ETFs covering virtually all segments of the market, including industry-specific, geographically focused, stock-capitalization segmented, and the like, and options trading is available on many of them. This allows for the building of a sophisticated portfolio even with lower amounts under management. No longer do you have to rely on active mutual fund managers who have no direct knowledge of your financial objectives, nor do you have to rely on a few broad-based ETFs like SPYs or DIAs.

For portfolios between $100,000 and $500,000, a combination of individual stocks and ETFs is advisable. If a particular sector looks as though it is becoming attractive due to price declines but is not an area in which you have expertise or the time to do proper research, ETFs allow you to participate without the risk of stock selection. The same holds true for geographical exposure. Most countries have only a limited number of securities that trade on the major U.S. exchanges via **American Depository Receipts (ADRs)** or **American Depository Shares (ADSs)**. Even if you could build a reasonable portfolio via a particular country's ADRs, you are often better off buying the 'S&P 500' of the country rather than selecting individual stocks. For example, if you want to get exposure to the Japanese market you can buy the EWJ ETF. Similarly, the XLYs will allow broad-based exposure to the discretionary consumer sector for those who think that this is a good segment in which to invest. The market can be sliced and diced in virtually any way via ETFs, making them an effective way to gain exposure to various segments without having to acquire enough individual securities to attain adequate diversification within that sector.

While there is no magic number, accounts of over $500,000 are generally large enough to merit exclusively individual securities;

however, you must consider whether you have sufficient time to do the research necessary to avoid fatal investment mistakes. ETFs mitigate individual stock purchase exposure risks. Thus, if your time to properly research and follow individual companies is limited and you still want to invest and trade actively (as opposed to buying index funds or actively managed mutual funds), you are well served using ETFs. That said, be certain that a given ETF is well diversified. For some ETFs, the top two or three holdings can represent 20% or more of the portfolio; in that case you are largely making an individual stock bet. However, the top ten portfolio holdings and their respective percentages of the total ETF makeup are easily researched, and most ETFs are fairly well diversified.

For option sellers and buyers, another consideration is whether options trade on a particular ETF. Not all ETFs have options associated with them, and even for those that do, often the volumes traded are so low that bid/ask spreads can be very wide. Examine closely options volumes and associated liquidity before placing orders. For options sellers, especially call sellers, this is less of a consideration in that if the bid is priced so that the amount of premium collected represents a good profit potential, then a wide spread is not that meaningful. For options purchasers looking to exit the transaction at a profit, though, wide bid/ask spreads can be a big inhibitor to profit generation even if your initial thesis is correct and the option price moves in the desired direction.

Another trade-off to using ETFs rather than individual stocks is that the diversification benefits inherently associated with ETFs are offset by their lower volatility and options premiums. By their nature, ETFs are less volatile than individual stocks, and accordingly the premiums a trader can get from selling options on ETFs will be less than he can receive for selling options on a similar basket of individual stocks.

## Number of Positions and Position Sizing

When it comes to portfolio construction and risk control, position sizing is an important element of optimizing the risk/reward profile. Generally, you should have twenty to thirty core long positions plus another five to ten special situations in your portfolio with the largest positions—those core holdings in which you have the greatest conviction—sized in the 3% to 5% range; special situations tend to be smaller position sizes. That said, anything less than a 1% or 2% position is typically not worth your while, whereas a single position should not be materially larger than 8%-10% and only of the highest quality. Given that some of your positions will likely be ETFs, a portfolio with twenty-five to forty positions will be more diversified than the number of positions suggests.

## POWER TIP
### Know the Score

At times, even with good liquidity in an option, spreads will be wide in both puts and calls. This is especially true when VIX is very high. You may have a spread on a call, for example, that is $2.70 X $3.50 on an option that under normal conditions has a spread of only $0.10. Your approach during these times is simple. First, always place limit orders rather than market orders as you might very well be able to get better than the bid for your order. Second, calculate your return profile and risk-reward ratio with the bid (or limit order) price in mind only. Do not worry about the high ask price; this is merely a function of extreme volatility. Finally, recognize that immediately after selling the option the position will be in a loss as the pricing for the position will reflect the higher ask. Again, this is not a concern because your profit profile is locked in. If you need to show period results (e.g., monthly or quarterly), then take this into consideration as you approach the end of a reporting period.

A portfolio with this number of total positions appears to be the ideal balance to allow for sufficient diversification and randomness of stock price relative to strike price at time of expiration while avoiding having so many positions that you cannot monitor them effectively.

The number of short option positions—calls and puts—will be dependent on your objectives. The active trader who uses the full spectrum of tools available will often have as many option positions as stock and ETF holdings, so that the entire portfolio has forty to sixty positions or more at any point in time. This might sound like a lot, but the typical mutual fund or ETF can have several hundred holdings.

In order to construct and oversee such a portfolio, you will need to research and analyze as well as monitor approximately seventy-five to one hundred companies at any given time.

In terms of industries, it is important not to allow any one industry segment to represent more than approximately 30% of your total portfolio. That said, generally stay agnostic as to industry preference. Instead, focus on the quality of the company, its fundamentals (including valuation), and its position and competitive strength within its industry.

**POWER TIP**
**Don't Get the Wrong Notion**

It is important to calculate your short put position size on a notional rather than delta adjusted basis for risk control purposes. There will be times when your short puts are way OTM and you will consider their effective position size to be negligible. This would be a mistake. You must make the assumption that your portfolio is subject to rapid and large declines, thus a delta adjusted 2% position by way of a short put can turn into a delta adjusted position of 8% very quickly as deltas accelerate in value due to a declining stock. Think early 2020 when the market declined over 30% in weeks and VIX spiked from the mid-teens to over 80. Your portfolio can go from being conservatively positioned to highly leveraged (by way of premature short put assignments) in a matter of days. Do the conservative, disciplined thing, which is to calculate short put option position sizes on a notional basis for risk control purposes.

**POWER TIP**
**Optimizing Dividend Reinvestment**

While the reinvestment of dividends can be one of the greatest sources of wealth accumulation, you are better served by taking your dividends in cash at times. Fortunately, with today's trading and portfolio-management tools, you can turn on and turn off the dividend reinvestment feature with a click of the mouse. In general, if you have purchased stock long and sold tight calls (near- or at-the-money), then dividends should not be reinvested as this position is meant for a near-term gain with the goal of getting assigned on the short call. In this case you are better off simply keeping the dividend in the form of cash rather than investing the cash for a small number of additional shares which you will be left with if your position is assigned.

However, if you have entered said position and the underlying stock goes down so that the short call expires worthless and you choose not to sell any additional short call premium (either because you cannot get enough premium without going too far out timewise, or you are fine with the position being a longer-term hold), then you are well served to have these and future dividends reinvested for potential capital gains. First, your position is intended for the long term. Second, the stock price is now far from the strike price at which you might be selling calls. Finally, the current stock price is lower than your entry point, and you are always better off buying more stock when it is low and selling stock (or buying less of it) when the price is high. You can reassess every few months whether you want the next quarter's dividends reinvested. Remember, you need to turn on or off the dividend reinvestment feature prior to the dividend being declared. If you wait until the stock has gone ex-dividend (but the payout has not yet been made), it will often be too late for your brokerage firm to execute your new instructions.

Whether your portfolio is predominantly ETFs, or stocks, or somewhere in the middle, you should have a solid, diversified representation of various industry and geographical sectors that are attractive investments or trades. (You do not need to have exposure to an industry just for the sake of diversification. If a particular sector or geographical region is overvalued in your opinion, you can pass on exposure in this area for now and wait until the investment opportunity is more compelling). At any point in time, some of your positions will be weak, some will be strong, and some will be middling. Many factors drive stock prices in the near term, some of them random (near-term noise) and some of them specific to the company or industry—for instance, macroeconomic news such as employment or interest rates, or company-specific fundamental news, like earnings announcements. Combine these ups and downs with the artificial construct of options expiration calendars, and for any given options cycle you will have some positions within your portfolio that close well below strike prices, some that are trading near-the-money, and others that are well ITM. With a well-constructed portfolio, you will have the opportunity regularly to make optimizing decisions about options moves vis-à-vis your stock and diversification to realize material gains over time.

## POWER TIP
### A Penny for Your Thoughts

There are times when you will want, if not need, to buy back options that are trading $0.00 X $0.05 for the sole purpose of freeing up margin availability. Though the option might be way OTM and about to expire worthless—and you would rather not spend the money to buy it back—it is worth doing if this frees up capital that allows you to sell other options. For example, if you are short way OTM Google puts leading up to expiration, these are likely to be eating into a great deal of margin equity. Thus, rather than selling stock, close this OTM option to free up buying (or option-selling) power to allow you to enter into a new, more profitable position.

Remember, a portfolio is a dynamic, organic entity; it is not a static stock pick. There are many variables to consider in constructing a portfolio that will serve you and your investing objectives well over time. You can be right in terms of stock selection and wrong in terms of investment management if you do not pay close attention to factors like position size, industry concentration, and hedging levels. Love each child individually, but do not forget that family dynamics are also vital to long-term success.

## Key Takeaways:

- Understand what the real investment risks are, starting with yourself.
- Portfolio construction should start with a financial plan to determine cash needs and time horizon. This will lead to asset allocation and security selection.
- ETFs can be a great way to express a low-cost diversified portfolio, but individual stocks can provide more flexibility and precision for larger accounts.
- Consider both core holdings and special situations when constructing your portfolio.
- There are myriad considerations beyond just stock selection for creating a superior portfolio; understand and implement these well.

# CHAPTER 7

## LESSONS LEARNED

When you have been involved in the stock market for decades and interacted with thousands of other investors with a wide range of investing styles, emotional make ups, and the like, you invariably learn many lessons (often the hard way). Here are some of the key ones that, if followed with discipline, should keep you out of trouble and increase the likelihood of investment success over time.

1. *Match your asset allocation with your time horizon.* The most important investment decision you can make is ensuring you invest your capital consistent with when you need the money back. This is also known as asset allocation. Need funds in the next 12 – 24 months? Then allocate to cash, money market funds, or short-term bonds, regardless of if stocks are in a bull, bear, or flat market (which as we know can change on a dime). Is money being invested for retirement five, 10, or more years hence? Then a well-diversified portfolio of high-quality stocks is in order. If you get this one decision right – and stick to it with discipline – then your chances of having a successful outcome will go up dramatically.

2. *Perform a financial plan.* The best way to determine your cash needs, time horizon, asset allocation, and investment plan is to work with a professional financial advisor to determine your balance sheet (think the picture) as well as your cash flow (think the movie). This process is invaluable both as a one-time process but also ongoing on an annual or as needed basis.

3. *Be patient.* This one seems obvious but like many things that are 'simple', it is not always easy to execute. When we are amid

a crisis, then time tends to slow down, and days of declining markets can feel like an eternity. By looking back at large market declines like the period of 2008-2009 or the winter/spring of 2020, you can reflect that in retrospect it did not take very long for stocks to recover. That perspective should give you more confidence and fortitude to be more patient the next time around.

4. *Never put yourself in a position where something must happen for the outcome to be successful.* Financial freedom is an admirable goal we should all strive to achieve. Being beholden to others is an uncomfortable feeling that smart investment decisions over time can alleviate. When you are constructing a portfolio, avoid situations where you are reliant on some type of short-term event (a stock trading to a certain level) for a successful outcome. Unless you are a full-time trader/investor, the time and stress associated with tracking time sensitive situations that are reliant on a specific outcome are simply not worth it. For example, if you are naked index calls that are in the money a day before expiration and you are counting on the fact that the market will drop the next day so that you don't end up short, this is a tenuous position to be in. Bottom line, construct your portfolio – and financial life – such that it can endure any foreseeable situation, and don't end up needing to act because you must as opposed to because you want to.

5. *Don't lose sight of the forest for the trees – or individual leaves.* Sometimes we get fixated on a given position and act as though it is a competition between us and the market. This can be especially true if we are trading options and trying to squeeze out every penny of profit. While it is certainly good to be detail oriented and competitive, make sure not to be penny wise and pound foolish. You may win the battle of a given position, but meanwhile you are losing troops right and left with major long positions. Bottom line, make sure to put everything in perspective. If you are long $100K of company X and this position is suffering, give it the proper attention versus being distracted by trying to earn the final $200 on a short call option.

6. *Turn your weakness into a strength.* It may sound counterintuitive but knowing (and acknowledging) a weakness can lead to a strength. Are you bad at budgeting? Work with your financial planner to create an actionable plan. Are you an emotional investor who watches CNBC every day? Create a plan with your financial advisor to determine your long-term goals. Agree on the plan and stick to it. Commercial airlines don't change the destination airport mid-flight.

7. *Don't complain about taking profits.* Whether it's a covered call option that's in the money and doesn't get rolled, or an individual stock that reaches a price target, it can be a good thing to take profits. Of course, it's always best to optimize taxes in the process, but the gift horse may be looking right at you.

8. *You can save and invest your way to retirement, but you can't allocate or trade your way there.* As important as asset allocation and portfolio management are, they will only get you to retirement if you have a good savings plan and sufficient assets to get there. Otherwise, you are just buying lottery tickets with the hopes of being able to retire. A comprehensive financial plan will ensure that all the ingredients (savings plan, asset allocation, and portfolio management) are in order to optimize your retirement.

9. *Implement the three-day rule.* With financial media screaming at us constantly, it can be tempting to enter a new position as soon as we hear about it or risk 'missing out.' Instead of falling prey to this temptation, follow the philosophy that it is more important to be right than quick when it comes to your investment dollars. Years later, it will not matter if you bought a stock a couple percentage points higher, but it will definitely make a difference if you are waiting to get to break even for a loser you never should have purchased. Bottom line, wait a few days between the time of considering entering into a given stock and actually pulling the trigger. Your future bank account will thank you.

# OTHER BOOKS BY SCOTT KYLE

*The Power Curve – Smart Investing Using Dividends, Options, and the Magic of Compounding*
thepowercuve.com

*Forever Young*
fynovel.com

*Via LaVie and the Friendship Code*
vialaviebooks.com

# ACKNOWLEDGMENTS

Any project of this magnitude is largely a team effort, and we owe great gratitude to the many people who were integral to its completion. Thanks first to Trystan Cleaver, Operations and Marketing Manager at Coastwise, for his invaluable assistance in creating the figures and charts contained in this book, as well as his work on the website www. thecompoundcode.com. Additional appreciation goes to the team at Conversion Publishing, especially Andrew Izumi for his guidance in the process. Thanks as well to Debbie O'Byrne and Teri Kojetin of JETLAUNCH for their excellent work on the cover and internal book design, respectively.

# GLOSSARY

**Active** An investment strategy in which the investor believes he can outperform the market by making specific investing and trading decisions. In business, someone who participates in the day-to-day operations and management of a company.

**American Depository Receipts (ADRs)** Since most other countries do not allow stock certificates to leave their borders, a foreign company may arrange for a trustee (typically a large bank) to issue ADRs (sometimes called American Depository Shares, or ADSs) that represent the actual, or underlying, shares. Each ADR is equivalent to a specific number of shares.

**American Depository Shares (ADSs)** A U.S. dollar–denominated equity share of a foreign-based company available for purchase on an American stock exchange. An ADS is issued by a depository bank in the U.S. under agreement with the issuing foreign company. An ADS is a single share of the entire issuance known as an ADR.

**American-Style Option** An option that can be exercised at any time by its owner.

**Annual Rates of Change (Per Share)** Compound yearly rates of change of per-share sales, cash flow, earnings, dividends, book value, or other industry-specific, per-share figures.

**Annual Total Return** A compound yearly return to shareholders that includes both stock price appreciation and dividend returns.

**Arbitrage** The process of buying an asset in one marketplace and concurrently selling it in another at a different price.

**Ask Price** The price at which someone is willing to sell a security. Alternatively, the price at which an investor can purchase a security.

**Assets** The total of current assets (normally cash and short-term investments, inventories, and receivables) and long-term assets (typically including property, equipment, and goodwill).

**Assignment** The process by which the investor is required to buy (in the case of a short put) or sell stock (in the case of being short a call) when options sold short are in-the-money at time of expiration. *See also* Called Away.

**At-the-Money (ATM)** Used to describe a call (or put) option that has a strike price equal to or near the price of the underlying asset.

**Average Annual Dividend Yield** Dividends declared per share for a year divided by the average annual price of the stock in the same year, expressed as a percentage.

**Average Annual Price/Earnings (P/E) Ratio** The average price of the stock for the year divided by earnings per share reported by the company for the year. *See also* Price/Earnings Ratio.

**Balance Sheet** A financial statement that lists a company's assets, debts, and owner's investment (shareholder equity) as of a specific date.

**Basis Point** One basis point equals one one-hundredth of one percentage point.

**Beta** A relative measure of the historical sensitivity of a stock's price to overall market fluctuations. A Beta of 1.50 describes a stock tends to rise (or fall) 50% more than the broad market.

**Bid Price** The price at which someone is willing to buy a stock or option contract, or conversely the price at which an owner of a stock or option can sell such security.

**Bond** A long-term debt instrument, typically characterized by fixed, semiannual interest payments and a specified maturity date.

**Book Value per Share** Net worth (including intangible assets), less preferred stock at liquidating or redemption value, divided by common shares outstanding.

**Buy to Close** The closing of an option contract, initiated by first selling short.

**Buy to Open** The act of initiating a contract position by buying a call or put.

**Buy Write** Buying a stock long while simultaneously selling a call against the long stock.

**Call Bear Spread** The simultaneous sale of a call at a given strike price and purchase of a call at a higher strike price.

**Call Bull Spread** The simultaneous purchase of a call at a given strike price and a sale of a call at a higher strike price.

**Call Option** An option which gives its buyer the right (but not the obligation) to buy a number of shares of an underlying security at a fixed price before a specified expiration date. Call buyers hope the price of the stock will rise. A call option can be sold as a way to generate income and/or provide some downside protection for a long position.

**Called Away** To be assigned, or required to sell, stock on which calls were sold short.

**Cash Flow** The total of net income plus noncash charges (depreciation, amortization, and depletion) less preferred dividends (if any).

**Cash-Settled Options** The owner of this type of option receives cash equal to the difference between the index's closing price and the strike price of the option rather than any securities. Most European-style options are cash based.

**CBOE** The Chicago Board Options Exchange.

**Chain (Option Chain)** An abbreviated means for providing relevant information for a given contract. Chains include the underlying security, the expiration date, the strike price, and the type of option (call or put).

**Compound Growth** The annual rate of growth of an investment when dividends or interest are reinvested.

**Contract** An exchange-traded derivative instrument that gives the holder of the contract the right, but not the obligation, to exercise the contract and trade the underlying asset at a specified price. In the case of equity options, each contract represents 100 shares.

**Core Holdings** A significant long-term position within a portfolio which is purchased with the intent of maintaining it for an extended period.

**Counterparty Risk** The risk that the other party in an agreement will default. This is also known as default risk.

**Covered** A position that is hedged.

**Covered Call** *See* Buy Write.

**Credit Spread** The difference between the amount received from selling an option and the amount paid for buying an option. The spread results in a credit when the price received for selling an option is higher than the price paid for buying the second option in the transaction.

**Current Asset** An asset on the balance sheet that might reasonably be expected to be converted into cash, sold, or consumed during the normal operating cycle of a business, usually twelve months or less. Current assets usually include cash, receivables, and inventory.

**Current Liabilities** Financial obligations that a business will have to satisfy within the next twelve months. Current liabilities include accounts payable, taxes, wage accruals, and total short-term debt, or debt due (the sum of notes payable and the portion of long-term debt maturing in the operating year).

**Current Ratio** The sum of current assets divided by the sum of current liabilities.

**Default Risk** *See* Counterparty Risk.

**Delta** The amount an option will change for a corresponding one-point change in the price of the underlying security. Delta values range from 0 to 1.0.

**Delta Adjusted Exposure** Gross, or notional, exposure for a given position multiplied by the position's delta.

**Delta Premium Credit** The additional premium received by virtue of closing one short option contract and selling a later-dated option with the same strike price.

**Depreciation** An amount charged against operating profits to reflect the aging of plant and equipment owned by a company.

**Dividend** A payout to shareholders determined by a board of directors.

**Dividend Declaration Date** The date a company declares a dividend payable in the future.

**Dividend Ex-Date** The date by which an investor must have purchased a stock in order to receive announced dividends or stock distributions. If the investor purchases stock on or after this date, he will not receive the dividend.

**Dividend Payment Date** The date a dividend is paid.

**Dividend Record Date** The date used to determine which shareholders are entitled to the dividend or distribution. This ensures that the dividend is sent to the correct people and credited to the correct accounts. The date is usually two business days after the ex-date.

**Dividend Yield** Total cash dividends declared over the previous twelve months, divided by the recent price of the stock.

**Dividends Paid per Share** The common dividends per share paid (but not necessarily declared) during the calendar year.

**Earnings** A company's total profit before nonrecurring gains or losses, but after all other expenses.

**Earnings per Share (EPS)** Net profits attributable to each common share as originally reported by the company but adjusted for all subsequent stock splits and stock dividends.

**Effective Yield** The current dividend divided by the original stock purchase price.

**Equity** Ownership interest held by shareholders in a corporation.

**European-Style Option** An option that can only be exercised on its expiration date.

**Exchange Traded Funds (ETFs)** A basket of stocks that trades throughout the day on a major exchange. Each ETF has a unique ticker and trades much like a regular stock.

**Exercise** To implement the rights of an option holder by buying (in the case of a call) or selling (in the case of a put) the underlying asset.

**Expiration Date** The date on which a contract ends.

**Exposure** The amount, or size, of a position. This can be represented in dollar or percentage terms, and on a notional or delta-adjusted basis, and as an absolute number or as a percentage of the total portfolio.

**Fill** The price at which an order is executed. To complete an order.

**Gamma** The rate at which delta changes.

**Gross Exposure** Total value of all positions (long and short) in a given portfolio position on a notional or face-value basis.

**Gross Long Exposure** Total value of all long-oriented positions (long equity, long calls, and short puts) on a notional or fully assigned basis.

**Gross Short Exposure** Total value of all short-oriented positions (short equity, long puts, and short calls) on a notional or fully assigned basis.

**Growth Stock** Stocks of companies with earnings that grow consistently and quickly over time, reflecting the fact that such companies have limited sensitivity to the country's economy as it moves up and down.

**Hedge** To enter a position that reduces the exposure or risk of an underlying position. To manage risk.

**Historical Volatility** A measure of a security's or index's past volatility, or change in price, over a given time period. Often measured by standard deviation over a preceding twelve-month period.

**Implied Volatility** A theoretical measure of a given security's or index's expected or imputed future volatility, usually over a thirty-day period.

**Income Statement** A financial report that lists revenues, expenses, and net income during a given period.

**Income Stocks** Equities with higher-than-average dividend yields (often, but not always, stocks with dividends that are likely to be maintained or raised).

**In-the-Money (ITM)** Used to describe a call (or put) option with a strike price that is less (or more in the case of a put) than the price of the underlying asset. If Company X common stock is trading at $25 per share, a call option on Company X with a strike price of $20 is in-the-money.

**Intrinsic Value** The value of a security, justified by factors such as assets, dividends, earnings, and management quality. Intrinsic value is at the core of fundamental analysis since it is used in an attempt to calculate the value in an individual stock and to then compare that value with the market price.

**Intrinsic Value Premium** The amount by which an option is in-the-money.

**Investor** Someone who allocates capital with a time horizon of a year or more with the objective of providing a return on that money.

**Last** The most recent price at which a trade was executed. In the case of illiquid securities and derivatives, this may differ substantially from current bid/ask quotes.

**Layer In** The process of entering less than the intended full position. For example, if your goal is to purchase 1,000 shares of Company X, you might purchase 500 shares today and wait for weakness to purchase the remaining 500 shares.

**LEAPS** Long-term equity anticipation securities. LEAPS are options that typically have expiration time frames of twelve months or longer.

**Leverage** The use of various financial instruments such as derivates (e.g., options, futures contracts) or margin borrowing with the goal of amplifying returns. In business, the use of borrowing (usually in the form of bank debt) to finance operations or to enhance ROE.

**Limit Order** An order placed to buy or sell a set number of shares or contracts at a specified price or better.

**Long** To enter a position with the objective of profiting from the increase in price of a security.

**Long-Term Debt** The portion of borrowings (including bank notes, debentures, and capitalized leases) that will be due not in the current twelve months, but in future operating years.

**Margin** An amount borrowed from one's brokerage firm.

**Market Capitalization (Market Cap)** The market value of all common shares outstanding for a company, calculated by multiplying the recent price of a stock by the number of common shares outstanding. While there is no single definition accepted, large-cap stocks typically have market values of more than $5 billion. Mid-cap stocks have market values from $1 billion to $5 billion. Small-cap stocks have market values of less than $1 billion.

**Market Neutral** A portfolio for which net exposure is at or near zero.

**Market Order** A buy or sell order in which the broker is to execute the order at the best price currently available.

**Market Value** The price at which a security currently can be sold.

**Multiple** A ratio, or measure, usually applied to various financial metrics of a company such as its earnings.

**Naked** To hold a position that is unhedged.

**Net Asset Value (NAV)** The market value of a company's assets less any liabilities divided by the number of shares outstanding. In the case of a mutual fund, the market value of all cash and securities held within the fund, less any liabilities, divided by the number of shares outstanding.

**Net Exposure** Gross long exposure less gross short exposure.

**Net Profit (or Income)** A company's total profit before nonrecurring gains or losses, but after all other expenses.

**Net Profit Margin** Net income before nonrecurring gains and losses as a percentage of revenues.

**Net Worth** All the assets shown on the balance sheet, including any tangible assets (i.e., goodwill, debt discount, deferred charges) less current liabilities, long-term debt, and all other noncurrent liabilities. In other words, the sum of common plus preferred stockholders' equity. Also referred to as shareholders' equity.

**Notional Exposure** The total face value of the option, were it fully assigned.

**Open Interest** The total number of contracts (for a given strike price and expiration period) that have not yet been exercised or expired or fulfilled by delivery. This is not the same as volume traded.

**Operating Earnings** Earnings left after subtracting the cost of goods sold, marketing, and general and administrative costs from sales. Sometimes referred to as EBITDA (earnings before interest, taxes, depreciation, and amortization).

**Option** A contract that gives the buyer the right to buy or sell 100 shares of stock within a certain period and at a pre-established price. A call option gives an investor a right to buy 100 shares of stock at a specified price, while a put option allows him to sell 100 shares.

**Out-of-the-Money (OTM)** Used to describe a call option with a strike price above the price of the underlying asset or a put option with a strike price below the price of the underlying asset. For example, a put option to sell 100 shares of Company X stock at $60 per share is out-of-the-money if the stock currently trades at $80. Even though an out-of-the-money option has no intrinsic value, it might have market value based on variables such as time and volatility.

**Passive** An investment strategy involving limited ongoing buying and selling of securities. A belief that one cannot outperform the market as a whole by taking advantage of near-term market fluctuations and/or the temporary mispricing of a given sector. In business, someone who does not play an active role in the management of a company.

**Payout Ratio** The ratio on a percentage basis of the net income a firm pays to its stockholders in dividends. If a company pays out no dividends, its payout ratio is 0%. If it pays out in dividends the exact amount of its earnings, its payout ratio is 100%. A company with earnings of $2 per share and an annual dividend of $1 per share has a payout ratio of 50%.

**Premium** The price at which an option trades. The size of the premium is affected by various factors including the time to expiration, interest rates, strike price, and the price and volatility of the underlying asset.

**Price** The amount at which any asset trades.

**Price/Earnings Ratio (P/E Ratio)** The most widely used measure of stock valuation. The price of the stock divided by earnings per share for a twelve-month period.

**Price/Earnings Growth Ratio (PEG)** The ratio of price/earnings per share compared to a company's growth rate. If a given company is trading for 22X earnings and its earnings are growing at 30% per year, its PEG ratio is approximately 0.73. In general, a PEG ratio under 1.0 is viewed as favorable.

**Price to Book** A stock's total capitalization (market cap) divided by its book value, calculated on either a total valuation or a per share basis.

**Price to Sales** A stock's total capitalization (market cap) divided by its sales over a twelve-month period.

**Put Bear Spread** The simultaneous purchase of a put at a given strike price and the sale of a put at a lower strike price.

**Put Bull Spread** The simultaneous sale of a put at a given strike price and purchase of a put at a lower strike price.

**Put Option** Gives the buyer the right to sell a number of shares of stock at a price until the option's expiration date. Put buyers hope the price of the stock will fall. Put options may be sold as a way to generate income and/or create an entry point for a stock purchase at a price that is lower than the then-market price of the stock.

**Ratio Call Selling** The sale of more short calls on a given position than what is held of long stock or deep in-the-money short puts.

**Raw** Gross, or total, return not converted to an annualized basis.

**Real Estate Investment Trust (REIT)** A financial intermediary that invests its equity capital and debt in income-producing real estate and mortgages. In general, at least 95% of otherwise taxable income must be distributed to shareholders in the calendar year earned, and specified percentages of both investments and gross income must be related to real estate.

**Retained Earnings** Net profit for the year, less all common and preferred dividends, when relating to the income statement. With respect to the balance sheet or common equity, it is the sum of net profit in all years of the company's existence, less all dividends (common and preferred) ever paid.

**Return on Equity (ROE)** A company's earnings divided by its shareholder equity. A critical measure that demonstrates how well a company uses its reinvested earnings to generate additional earnings.

**Return on Investment (ROI)** For a business, a measure of a company's profitability for a given time period, usually twelve months, divided by total common stock, preferred equity, and long-term debt. How effectively a company uses its capital to produce profits. For investors, the amount of money made divided by the capital deployed for a given investment.

**Roll** To close one option contract and open up a new contract with the same strike price but a later-dated expiration.

**Roll Up and Out** To close one option contract and open a new contract with a higher strike price (in the case of a call) and a later-dated expiration.

**Sales** Gross volume less returns, discounts, and allowances; net sales.

**Sell to Close** To complete a contract position that was opened up by buying long.

**Sell to Open** The act of initiating an option contract by first selling it short.

**Sell Write** To sell a stock short while simultaneously selling a put against the short stock position.

**Settlement Price** The price established by the exchange at the end (or beginning in the case of index options) of each day for the purposes of determining net gains or losses in a given contract as well as margin requirement.

**Shareholder's Equity** A balance sheet item showing net worth less the liquidating or redemption value of any preferred issues outstanding. Represents the sum of the value of common stock at par, the surplus of capital received (over par value), and retained earnings (i.e., earned surplus). Retained earnings are the sum of net profits earned in all years less dividends paid in all years.

**Short** To enter a position with the objective of profiting from the decline in the price of a security.

**Short Hedge** An investment transaction that is intended to provide protection against a decline in the value of an asset. For example, an investor who holds shares of General Motors and expects the stock to decline might enter into a short hedge by purchasing a put option on GM stock. If GM does subsequently decline, the value of the put option would increase.

**Special Situations** Otherwise high-quality companies that pay little or no dividends and, temporarily and for nonfundamental reasons, have fallen on hard times.

**Spread** The difference, or delta, between the bid and the ask.

**Standard Deviation** A measure of a security's volatility, usually calculated over a twelve-month period. The distance a stock is likely to move from its average.

**Stock Dividend** The issuance of additional common shares to common stockholders, with no change in total common equity. From an accounting standpoint, retained earnings (i.e., the earned surplus) are reduced and the value of the reported common stock component of common equity (usually called the par value account) is increased.

**Straddle** The purchase or sale of puts and calls in equal proportion and with the same terms.

**Strangle** The purchase of both an out-of-the-money put and an out-of-the-money call, each option having the same underlying asset and maturity.

**Strike Price** The exercise price at which the owner of a call option can purchase the underlying stock or the owner of a put option can sell the underlying stock.

**Synthetic Stock** A financial instrument that artificially simulates another instrument through the combination of other assets. For example, the simultaneous purchase of a long call and the sale of a short put creates a synthetic stock.

**Tau** *See* Vega.

**Theta** The measurement of time decay of a given option position.

**Time Value Premium** Total premium less intrinsic value premium. In the case of out-of-the-money options, the entire premium amount is time value premium.

**Total Exposure** *See* Gross Exposure.

**Trader** Someone who allocates capital with a time frame of one year or less with the goal of getting a return on that capital.

**Value** The amount of an asset's true worth based on objective financial metrics.

**Vega** The amount by which the option price changes when volatility changes.

**VIX** The implied volatility for the S&P 500 for the subsequent thirty-day period.

**Volatility** The measure of the amount by which an underlying security is expected to fluctuate in a given period.

**Volume** The total number of shares or options traded over a given period, usually a day.

**VXN** The implied volatility for the NASDAQ 100 for the subsequent thirty-day period.

**Working Capital** The amount of current assets found on the balance sheet, less current liabilities.

**Write** To sell an option. The seller of the option is known as the writer of the option.

**Yield** Dividends paid for the previous twelve months divided by the current price, expressed as a percentage.

# INDEX

Made in United States
Orlando, FL
11 June 2023

34052357R00114